Mountain
BIKE

MAGAZINE'S
COMPLETE GUIDE TO

Mountain
Biking
Skills

Mountain BIKE

MAGAZINE'S COMPLETE GUIDE TO

Mountain Biking Skills

Expert Tips on Conquering Curves, Corners, Dips, Descents, Hills, Water Hazards and Other All-Terrain Challenges

By the Editors of **Mountain BIKE** and *Bicycling* Magazines

Rodale Press, Inc.
Emmaus, Pennsylvania

Copyright © 1996 by Rodale Press, Inc.
Cover photograph copyright © 1996 by Walter Smith
Illustrations copyright © 1996 by William Nealy

Library of Congress Cataloging-in-Publication Data

Mountain bike magazine's complete guide to mountain biking skills: expert tips on conquering curves, corners, dips, descents, hills, water hazards and other all-terrain challenges / by the editors of Mountain Bike and Bicycling magazines
    p.   cm.
  Includes index.
  ISBN 0-87596-300-5   paperback
  1. All Terrain cycling. I. Mountain Bike (1990) II. Bicycling.
GV1056.M68   1996
796.6–dc20   95–37285

Distributed in the book trade by St. Martin's Press

2   4   6   8   10   9   7   5   3   paperback

—— OUR MISSION ——

We publish books that empower people's lives.

—— RODALE ▣ BOOKS ——

Mountain Bike Magazine's Complete Guide to

Mountain Biking Skills

Editorial Staff

MANAGING EDITOR: SHARON FAELTEN
SENIOR EDITOR, MOUNTAIN BIKE MAGAZINE:
   BETH STRICKLAND
EDITORS: LEE JACKSON, JULIA VANTINE
WRITERS: HANK BARLOW, TIM BLUMENTHAL,
   DON CUERDON, JAY DEJESUS, GEOFF DRAKE,
   ZAPATA ESPINOZA, BOB HOWELLS, JOE KITA,
   DAN KOEPPEL, JOHN KUKODA, SCOTT MARTIN,
   JOHN OLSEN, HANS REY, OLIVER STARR,
   BETH STRICKLAND, BILL STRICKLAND
ASSOCIATE ART DIRECTOR: DEBRA SFETSIOS
STUDIO MANAGER: JOE GOLDEN
BOOK AND COVER DESIGNER: CHRISTOPHER R. NEYEN
MANAGING PHOTO EDITOR: SUSAN POLLACK
PHOTO EDITOR: LIZ REAP
COVER PHOTOGRAPHER: WALTER SMITH
INTERIOR ILLUSTRATOR: WILLIAM NEALY
COPY EDITOR: KATHY DIEHL
PRODUCTION MANAGER: HELEN CLOGSTON
MANUFACTURING COORDINATOR: PATRICK T. SMITH
OFFICE STAFF: ROBERTA MULLINER, JULIE KEHS,
   BERNADETTE SAUERWINE, MARY LOU STEPHEN

RODALE HEALTH AND FITNESS BOOKS

VICE-PRESIDENT AND EDITORIAL DIRECTOR:
   DEBORA T. YOST
ART DIRECTOR: JANE COLBY KNUTILA
RESEARCH MANAGER: ANN GOSSY YERMISH
COPY MANAGER: LISA D. ANDRUSCAVAGE

C O N T

ENTS

Part 3: Advanced Skills

Part 4: Dealing with the Elements

Part 5: Tips from the Pros

Part 6: Ready for Racing

Introduction

Most of us learned how to ride a bike early in life. There was that day when you were five or six that your parents ran alongside you shouting instruction and encouragement while you frantically pedaled and tried to remember all you'd been taught. Then you wrecked. But you jumped back on, learning from your mistake. Then you wrecked again. And you learned again. And wrecked, and learned...

This went on for an entire afternoon, until finally, gratefully, everything clicked. Your bike stayed upright, you pedaled and braked with ease, you were smiling, your parents were beaming. You had learned to ride a bike. The hard part was over.

Get ready for "Hard Part Revisited." Knowing how to ride a bike on the road doesn't mean you'll be able to take a mountain bike on the trail with the same ease. Riding a mountain bike on a log-strewn singletrack requires skills your parents probably didn't teach you that day long ago. That's what this book is for.

You'll find chapters on choosing the right bike, basic and advanced riding skills, how to ride in any weather and tips from professional mountain bikers. Along the way, you may get frustrated, you'll undoubtedly crash, you'll want to quit, and you'll quite likely even cry.

But eventually, with dedication and practice, that magical feeling from your childhood will return. Only this time, your mother won't be there.

Beth Strickland

Senior Editor, <u>Mountain Bike</u> Magazine

Part 1 Starting

Out

HIT THE DIRT ①

By Bill Strickland

've never had my chain sucked. I think. It's hard to be sure. In ten years of road riding—during which, by the way, I sucked many a wheel—I thought I'd mastered cycling jargon.

That's until the guy on the mountain bike in front of me veers away from the plank bridge that connects our foot-wide trail with another and aims his bike into the muddy rip in the earth that necessitates the bridge's existence.

My best-case guess is that the free fall into the trench might shellac him with enough ooze to keep his legs from breaking. But the guy—this is a big guy, 200-plus pounds—gets his bike to hop the hole, stay upright, stay on the trail and begin scooting up the incline on the other side.

Me? I've shut down. My brakes are clamped, and my mouth is wide open. This position must align my facial features in the optimal sonic arrangement, because even though my mind is preoccupied with the display of finesse and force, I clearly hear when the rider stops at the top of the hill and says "Chainsuck."

I don't know if that's an insult, an invitation or an explanation. All I know for sure is that I couldn't get across that gully if I practiced for 30 years—and yet I want to try it right now.

SANS PAVEMENT

Like all the best things in life, mountain biking scares the hell out of you and seduces you at the same time. This is true especially if you're a beginner.

I'm a fat-tire tyro, a know-nothing wanna-be, an off-road rebel without a clue. But so what? In this sport, ignorance really can be bliss. This is my first real ride sans pavement since I was 15. Even though I can't speak the language and have already fallen (and fallen behind) more than in my past 100 road rides, and even though I did this weird sliding somersault sort of move in a wide dusty turn and ripped a hole in my cycling shorts and kind of twisted my ankle, I'm having more fun than I've had on a bike since . . . well, since I was 15.

I can't sling the slang yet, but I think I'm getting "thrashed." I know I'm happy. And hooked.

And ready to learn more. If you're still reading, I suspect you're a lot like me. You got a taste of this sport somewhere, and you're ready to chow. You just don't know which fork to use, or how to hop gullies or maybe not even how to ride in a straight line.

You might be an experienced road rider ready for something new. Or maybe you own a mountain bike, or a quasi-mountain bike, but have never taken it farther off-road than the sidewalk. Maybe your first fat-tire experience discouraged you because it was either on too-tough singletrack (a narrow trail) or over boring wide dirt roads.

NEWCOMER'S VERTIGO

I've already made what will doubtless be my largest leap of improvement. It's as easy as going on that first roadless ride and not letting the initial ten minutes of newcomer's vertigo discourage you. Once you're past that, you automatically become better. Incredibly better.

During my initial trail trial, I was so wobbly I thought I was teetering on one wheel instead of two. The soft surface of the path seemed to shift under my tires like brown Jell-O, and I banged into every bump possible. Streams, trees, bushes, rock outcroppings. Even flowers weren't attractions—they were obstacles.

My body was off-road, but my head was still road riding. The riders I was with explained that it's a matter of acclimation, of getting used to this strange world where the gravity as well as the ground is a little different. They gave me two pieces of advice, and for those first ten minutes, I repeated them to myself like mantras.

Just relax. The chief physical demand of mountain biking resembles the lifestyle of the sport's best riders: hang loose. If you feel you have to concentrate on anything, concentrate on not concentrating—at least until you know what you should be doing. Until then, ride by instinct. This may sound like a Zen/Yoda thing, and maybe it is, but there are some real practical applications, too.

One of my biggest mistakes, for instance, was trying to avoid too many things. On the road, objects protruding from the pavement are so rare and shocking that the lead rider in a group points to help everyone behind avoid them. On the trail, no rider could point to all the rocks, logs, branches, puddles and other stuff.

But that's no problem because you don't have to avoid every obstacle. Mountain bikes are designed to go over most things without tipping or slipping. Once you realize that twigs and pebbles aren't dangerous, your eye ignores all 908 of them littering the trail and looks only for significant objects. Since your steering follows your vision, your front tire stops chicken-scratching and settles into what's called a smoother "line." The result is that your control and balance improve.

Just ride. Every time I watched the rider in front of me execute some fancy hop, twist or slide, I thought "Uh-oh, I can't do that. Time to dismount and walk."

But one time I accidentally rode into one of those rock paths before I could stop. I bit the side of my cheek, hung onto the handlebar and kept pedaling. Went right over it. Not gracefully, but successfully.

Impressive off-road acrobatics may be the best way over obstacles, but they aren't the only way.

Beginners often approach obstacles too slowly, bringing the bike nearly to a stop while deciding the next move. This adds the difficulty of balancing a nearly stationary bike. It also makes the rider begin from a stop instead of using the momentum that's needed to surmount most challenges. I improved the most when I began riding just a little faster than I felt comfortable doing. Try it. You'll clear and climb things that will boggle you. You'll wish you could have seen yourself.

Before I accepted these two pieces of advice, I was a road rider on a funny bike. Now I'm a mountain biker. Maybe not a good one yet, but at least I feel like I belong out there.

You do, too. Go out and live through those first ten off-road minutes if you haven't already. You'll have a blast. You can't help it when you're off-road on a mountain bike. I know. I just found out.

HAVE A FIT ②

By John Kukoda

Being comfortable and confident on the trail is essential to becoming a better mountain biker. But being comfortable and confident on the bike is critical. A bike that fits will do more for your riding than that new shifting system or fancy brakes. So make sure you're riding the correct bike. Use the following outline and the photo on page 6 as a guide.

1. Frame. For the quick dismounts of off-road riding, you need lots of clearance between you and the top tube. The ideal mountain bike size is about 2 to 4 inches smaller than your road bike size. This isn't as critical if you will be riding only on pavement or smooth dirt roads, but there's no advantage to having a frame that's any larger than the smallest size that provides enough saddle height and reach to the handlebar. Smaller frames are lighter, stiffer and more maneuverable.

Manufacturers specify frame size in different ways. All start at the center of the crank axle and measure along the seat tube. But some stop at the center of the top tube, others go to its top and a few use the top of an extended seat lug. Plus, many mountain bikes have sloping top tubes and correspondingly short seat tubes. In this situation, it's possible for a 15- or 16-inch mountain bike (as measured by seat tube length) to be the ideal size for someone who rides a 22- or 23-inch road bike.

2. Saddle height. Seatpost lengths of 350 mm (about 14 inches) or more are common, so a lot can be out of the frame before the maximum extension line shows. For efficient pedaling, your knee should remain slightly bent at the bottom of the pedal stroke (the same as with a road bike). However, you may wish to lower the saddle slightly for rough terrain, enabling the bike to float beneath you without pounding your crotch. On steep descents, some riders like to drop the saddle even farther to keep their weight low and rearward, but others just slide off the back. A narrow saddle helps this technique.

3. Saddle tilt. Most riders prefer a level saddle, but some (including many women) find a slight nose-down tilt avoids pressure and irritation. Others go slightly nose-up, which helps them sit back and lessen strain on their arms. If the saddle has a raised nose and tail with recessed center, lay a straightedge from end to end to determine tilt.

4. Fore/aft saddle position. Your saddle is not positioned to match your reach to the handlebar—that's why stems come with different extensions. It's related to the pedal axle. Use the same procedure that roadies do: When seated comfortably with crankarms horizontal, a plumb line dropped from the bump just below your forward kneecap should bisect the pedal axle. Slide the saddle to achieve this. Riders who specialize in hill climbs sometimes put their saddles far-

If the bike fits, ride it: Here's a guide to a perfect fit.

ther forward so they can sit on the comfortable part of the seat rather than the narrow nose when hunched over the bar. A bike set up this way should have a correspondingly longer stem to avoid a cramped upper body.

5. Stem height and rise. For good control, the stem should place the bar an inch or two below the top of the saddle. This helps put weight on the front wheel so it's easier to steer on climbs and less likely to pull up. Lower is even better, but it can be scary on descents. Never exceed the stem's maximum extension line or it could break and cause a crash.

6. Handlebar width. An end-to-end measurement of 21 to 24 inches is common. If the bar seems too wide for comfort, it can be trimmed with a hacksaw or pipe cutter. First, though, move your controls and grips inward and take a ride to make sure you'll like the new width. And remember to leave a bit extra at each end if you use bar-ends. In general, the narrower the handlebar, the quicker the steering. Wider bars provide more control at slow speed.

7. Handlebar sweep. Flat bars can be straight or have up to 11 degrees or so of rearward bend per side. The choice is strictly one of arm and wrist comfort. Be aware that changing the sweep also changes your reach to the grips and could require a different stem length.

8. Bar-ends. These attachments (not shown) provide extra hand positions for cruising and climbing. When you're standing to pedal, they allow a grip akin to holding the brake hoods of a drop-bar road bike. In the saddle, they stretch the upper body when you're perched on the nose during steep ascents. Angle them slightly upward. Models that curve inward help protect the hands and are less likely to snag brush on tight singletrack. If you're thinking of adding bar-ends, make sure your handlebar can accept them; some ultralight models can't.

9. Top tube and stem length. Add these dimensions to determine handlebar reach. When choosing among various frame sizes that allow your correct saddle height (thanks to long seatposts), use the combined top tube and stem lengths to decide. You want comfortably bent arms and a straight back. A longer and lower reach works for fast cruising, but a higher, closer hand position affords more control on difficult trails. Once the saddle's fore/aft position is set, you can fine-tune your reach by selecting a stem extension from about 8 to 15 cm.

10. Crankarm length. Manufacturers usually vary this with frame size. For greater leverage on steep climbs, mountain bikes typically come with crankarms that are 5 mm longer than those of road bikes for the same size rider.

11. Arms. Slightly bent arms act as shock absorbers. If you can only reach the bar with elbows locked, get a shorter stem and/or condition yourself to lean forward more. If your upper arms and shoulders fatigue quickly when riding, you may need a longer stem or even a frame with a longer top tube. If your lower back usually aches, the reach might be too long.

12. Back. When your top tube/stem length combo is correct, you should have a forward lean of about 45 degrees during normal riding. This is the most efficient angle because the strong gluteus muscles of the buttocks don't contribute much to pedaling when you're sitting more upright. Plus, a forward lean shifts some weight to the arms so your butt doesn't get as sore.

13. Upper body. Don't hunch your shoulders and you'll avoid muscle soreness and fatigue. Retilt your head every few minutes to stave off tight neck muscles.

14. Hands and wrists. Grasp the bar just firmly enough to maintain control. Set the brake levers close to the grips and angle them so you can extend a finger or two around each and still hold the bar comfortably. Always ride with your thumbs under the bar so your hands won't slip on a bump. On rough terrain, grip more firmly for safety and use bent arms to absorb bouncing. Firm grips are less fatiguing to the hands than the squishy ones that feel so nice on the showroom floor.

YOUR FIRST 100 DAYS ③

By Dan Koeppel

You want a new bike. Hey, who doesn't? But deciding where to go and what to buy can be tough. You have mountains of information to wade through: catalogues, magazines, friends' recommendations, bike shop salespeople. And there's more to bike ownership than just buying a bike. You also need to consider which accessories you need, which trails to ride and how to maintain your new rig.

Beginners are often overwhelmed with all this data, so we've outlined a basic 100-day process to help you in your quest. (You won't be riding every day, so the days aren't consecutive.) None of these rules are hard-and-fast—if you simply want to ignore them, buy a rig and hit the dirt this afternoon, go for it. This is an arbitrary guide that isn't intended to be followed exactly (and it will drive you crazy to try). Instead, use it for inspiration and add your own ingredients—speed, friends, sight-seeing, whatever—to the mix.

In this guide we frequently refer you to your local shop for advice and guidance. These face-to-face encounters with skilled riders—which every shop should have—are still the best way to become a happy, competent mountain biker. Special bonus if your shop has an espresso bar. We begin on a Sunday. . . .

DAY 1

In three weeks you're going to buy a bike. The first step is to identify your price range. Real mountain bikes—the kind you can ride on singletrack and dirt—start at about $500. For around $700, you can get a bike with personality that will serve you well as your skills build on more technical terrain. Higher-level, race-ready mountain bikes start at about $1,000.

DAY 2

Today, you'll choose a frame material. Most bikes are made of steel, aluminum, carbon fiber or titanium. Rigs less than $1,000 are usually steel or aluminum. How do you choose the material that's best for you?

Steel is in theory more durable, but heavier. Many riders find that steel is more comfortable. It is a more forgiving metal, so it absorbs more shock. Aluminum is stiffer, so it is faster, but it leaves you feeling a little more beat up. Younger riders rarely seem to mind. Aluminum bikes are also lighter than steel. Titanium bikes are generally more comfortable and lighter—and even a mid-priced one costs more than $2,300. And although Ti bikes won't corrode and there's no paint to chip, buyers have no color option—just a silver-gray finish. Carbon fiber rigs are also extremely light and can be costly, with a median price of around $1,800.

DAY 3

What kind of bike should I buy? Here are some broad categories.

Good Times. If you're looking for relaxed fun—with a few excursions onto mild dirt—you can spend as little as $400 and get a good rig. For those four bills, you get a steel bike without suspension, with 21-speed gearing and a relatively heavy weight of about 30 pounds. 'Good Times' bikes rarely have high-performance tires or lightweight components.

What's Happenin'. You want to ride off-road, but you're not necessarily a racer. Instead, you dream of long days, plundering, thundering and blundering through beautiful forests and streams and mountains and valleys—or city streets at high speed. At $700 and up, you'll find plenty of bikes to suit you. Among the variables: braze-ons for extra water bottles and racks (great for touring); suspension; Grip Shift (a throttle-type gear-shifting system) or Shimano Rapidfire (push-button–type shifters). We've generally found Grip Shift to be easier to learn, but Shimano set-ups have a better initial shifting feel. Bikes for this type of usage are often made of steel or aluminum, though some pricey ones are titanium.

The Jeffersons. If you're moving up, you want a race-ready bike. Race bikes almost always have front suspension. They're usually made of aluminum or metal matrix composite (a stronger, stiffer, aluminum-based alloy). Carbon fiber and thermoplastic frames also fall into this category. Race bikes usually have Shimano's LX, XT or XTR parts group, though there may be many substitutions of rarer, trickier, custom parts. Some race bikes have suspension on the front and rear. These bikes are called softtail rigs, and they vary widely in ride quality and function—some are for downhill only; others are for cross-country riding. Most good ones are pretty pricey.

That's My Mama. More bike manufacturers are offering bikes specifically for women. That's a good thing. Women's bikes fall into the same three categories already described but feature smaller frame sizes, shorter top tubes, wider women's saddles and other specially sized components such as grips. If you ask at a bike shop for a women's bike and they show you an old-style girl's bike—or steer you toward the cheapo section—smile demurely and remind the dinosaur that 55 percent of adult bike riders are women.

DAY 7 (WEEKEND)

If you have a bike—any kind of a bike—go for a ride. Enjoy it. Find out what you like and don't like about your current bike. Does it make your body hurt? Is the shifting easy? Does the bike smooth out the road, or do you feel every bump? Keep this in mind for your test rides.

DAY 9

Suspension or not? At the $700 range, you can choose a bike with a suspension fork—or without. It's up to you, but we generally recommend that riders drop seven bills on a non-sprung bike. Why? It isn't that we don't like suspension; it's an off-road essential. But suspension forks are costly, and if you buy a $700 bike that has one, the manufacturer probably had to cut corners elsewhere—in parts selection or in the quality of the fork or frame—to make the price point. Get the best bike you can without suspension, then save about $300 for a good suspension fork.

DAY 11

Prepare for an upcoming weekend bike shop visit. Locate the shops in your town. Compile a "possible candidates" list of bikes. Most bike shops sell three or four brands, so you won't find every candidate at every shop. Unless you already have a favorite shop, plan on visiting two to four local dealers.

DAY 13

Here's what to look for in a bike shop. The most important thing—more important than slick displays, cut-rate prices or having all the latest accessories and toys—is service. A good bike shop such as Moab, Utah's, famed Rim Cyclery, has a staff that knows bikes, rides bikes, loves bikes. They'll talk to you about your needs and make recommendations beyond what a printed buyer's guide can. When you visit shops this weekend, this is what you'll be looking for. If you find a shop like this, buy your bike there. A mutation of the breed is the snob-geek bike shop. These folks ride bikes and know bikes, but act like you're a fool. You can either avoid these shops or do them a favor by saying: "It's going to be hard for me to buy a bike here unless you explain this stuff to me with a little more patience and respect."

DAY 15 (WEEKEND)

Don't buy a bike today. Instead, spend the day getting to know the bike shops you've chosen, finding your correct bike size and checking a few rigs. Size is absolutely critical—and it varies widely. Usually, you want about four inches of clearance—space between your crotch and the bike's top tube when you are straddling it. If possible, have the shop determine your size with a Fit Kit.

Beginner's note: Many first-timers tend to pick bikes that are too big for them. Avoid this temptation—if the bike feels too small and you haven't ridden for ten years, it may not be. Once you've determined your size, start checking individual models.

DAY 17

You have a list of bikes and a list of bike shops. Now try to narrow your choice down to three or four bikes.

DAY 18

Come up for air. Spend some time with family, friends or your local cable operator.

DAY 19

The weekend's coming up, and you're ready to do some test-riding. For most bike shops, this means a pretty limited parking lot jaunt. These can help determine little more than fit and saddle comfort—important, but not always reliable indicators of a bike's off-road worthiness. So today, call your mountain bike friends and arrange, for this weekend, a real ride on a borrowed bike, preferably a pretty new model. Say these words: "Take me on a very easy trail. Don't kill me."

DAY 20

Your warm-up ride. The object is to have fun and get the feel of a bike on dirt—so you'll know what you like and hate about today's bikes before you buy. If you don't know how to shift, this is a good time to learn. How? Simple: shifting either makes pedaling easier (for climbing hills) or harder. Harder pedaling makes you go faster on flats and descents. Modern gears are pretty bulletproof, so the best way to learn to shift is to just go wild: keep changing gears, be attentive to what's comfortable and don't mind the horrific grinding sounds. The goal? Comfortable, smooth pedaling.

DAY 21 (SATURDAY)

Visit your chosen bike shops again. Take each bike on your list for a test ride. Follow one of these two chosen methods.

Enlightened/controversial. We recommend rigorous off-road or parking lot tests of bikes. We wish more bike shops would offer real test rides on selected rigs for interested customers. But there are good reasons some don't. It can be expensive, dangerous and legally questionable. Still, you have a right to ask for a real test ride—and we think dealers should develop test-ride programs, if at all possible. If your shop does offer a test ride, you should be able to spend an hour on your chosen bike, determining how comfortable it feels and how well it climbs, descends, handles and stops. You might be able to take the bike on a stretch of dirt to do this. Criteria? If you're testing bikes head-to-head, use your instincts: The bike that feels best to you—provided it has been properly sized—is the one you should choose.

Conservative/safe. The "feels best" rule works here, too. But you'll be able to do little more than scoot the bike around the parking lot. Take at least 15 minutes on each bike. Do some turns and stops. Ride over a speed bump. Judge how good it all feels: Do any parts of your body hurt or feel strained? That's a sign of possible bad fit. Does the bike feel nimble or sluggish? Can you feel the bumps in the pavement—or do they seem to vanish beneath you? Finally, stand and sprint. Does the bike feel like it "squirts" forward—or does it feel flexible and slow?

When you're back in the shop, ask the dealer to again explain the differences between the bikes you've chosen. Ask about frame materials and parts groups. If they're different, ask about the advantages of each. Then ask the dealer to weigh each bike for you. Insist on this. Most of the bikes you're riding will tip the scales between 24 and 30 pounds. Those pounds make huge differences, and average-size riders should generally go for lighter bikes. Bigger riders might choose slightly heavier models for durability.

Now, go home. You're going to sleep on it. Think about the bike you chose. Did it feel right? Comfortable? Tomorrow, you're going to go back to the bike shop and make a deal. That means spending some money—and asking more questions.

DAY 22 (SUNDAY)

Today's the day to buy the bike. By now, you've chosen a good shop and a good rig. You may feel the temptation to bargain, to ask for some "throw-ins." Dealers generally won't bargain on low- to mid-range bikes because they can't afford to. Profit margins for these bikes are notoriously slim. When you consider shipping, assembly and free tune-up costs, most shops are making less than $100 on a $500 bike. One thing you should certainly ask for is fixes on anything you didn't like. Uncomfortable saddle? Have it changed. You should get a trade-in discount. What about extras, such as water bottles or pumps? You can usually get the shop to throw in a bottle and cage, but higher-end items (such as pumps and helmets) will be harder to bargain for. Ask the shop about a package deal for necessary accessories.

Take advantage of the free 30-day tune-up most shops offer for new bikes. Some dealers also offer extended warranties, much like those sold with appliances. Before buying such a contract, be sure you're not duplicating the manufacturer's warranty and that you truly need such insurance. Bikes are simple, sturdy machines, and in many cases, the extra money might be better spent on accessories.

Before you leave the shop, make sure you have these essential items: helmet, shorts, pump, spare tube and repair kit. If you're new to cycling and you don't know how to fix a flat, ask the dealer to show you. He shouldn't grouse about spending time doing this if you've just plunked down hundreds of raspberries. Also ask the dealer to fit the helmet for you, show you how to use the front-wheel quick-release and demonstrate how to release the front brake cable. You can usually get these quickie lessons while the bike is being assembled. Total cost for these essential accessories: about $150.

Other items you might consider: shoes ($50 and up), jersey ($30 and up), gloves ($15 and up), local trail map ($5 and up), seat bag ($15 and up), trail bell ($5 and up), multipurpose tool ($20 and up), repair manual ($15 and up), speedometer ($20 and up), energy bars ($1 and up) and car rack ($30 to $500). One note: If your shop tends to get busy on weekends, you may want to postpone your purchase until a weekday, when you might get superior attention.

Relieve the stress of maxing out your Visa by going for a ride. We recommend a shakedown cruise—if you feel safe, ride home from the shop. Pay attention to traffic and just ride. Don't get distracted by all the newfangled stuff you have. If you're the type who does get distracted, throw the bike in the trunk and head to your nearest bike path. Your first ride should be pure fun. Noodle around. Enjoy yourself. Get the feel of your bike.

DAYS 23 TO 26

Your first week with your bike. Practice fixing a flat. Practice with the front wheel quick-release. Ride around the block or on the bike path a few times. Most important? Find a trail to ride this weekend. How? The bike shop should know. Or call a local park and ask if mountain bikes are allowed. Become familiar with the International Mountain Bicycling Association's (IMBA) "Rules of the Trail."

- Ride on open trails only.
- Leave no trace.
- Control your bicycle.
- Always yield trail.
- Never spook animals.
- Plan ahead.

DAY 29 (WEEKEND)

During the past week, you've ridden a couple of times: on the bike path, around your block. Now it's time to get dirty (if you haven't already). Prepare the night before by filling two water bottles and packing your seat bag with your inner tube, tire irons, multipurpose tool, identification, money (including change) and an energy bar or two. It's preferable—but not always practical—to ride to the trail. Riding or driving, get yourself there by 10:00 A.M.

Your goal is to have fun, learn a few skills and not die. If you're a beginner, the most important thing you can learn is balance. Try to shift and pedal smoothly. Climbing, descending and getting over obstacles in mountain biking are largely matters of shifting your weight. Try weight shifting by moving your body forward and backward, up and down. Imagine someone is pressing your shoulders down. This weights the front wheel and helps on steep climbs. Imagine that your shoulders are weightless and your body shifts back, giving you rear-wheel traction. Relax on the bike and have a good time.

DAY 30

Your bike is filthy from yesterday. Don't sweat it. Be proud. It's a good idea to wash the mud off your bike as soon as you can after the ride before the mud gets hard. Use a very light, diffuse spray to whisk mud away, keeping water away from bearings and seals because a direct hit will penetrate almost any seal. When water gets past a seal, that bearing will be toast in a few days. Use a sponge and a bucket of warm, soapy water to make the frame and rims shiny and new again. Be sure to get all the black grunge buildup off the braking surfaces on the rims, or your brakes won't work well the next time you ride. When your bike is dry, lube your chain with Tri-Flow.

DAYS 31–35

Plan a more ambitious ride, in the ten-mile range. Your goal is to find a "local." That's a trail you can ride regularly, building your skills as you gain experience. Look for a trail with some climbing, some descending, some pavement (for smooth pedaling) and some challenge: maybe a water crossing or some singletrack.

DAY 36 (WEEKEND)

Ride your local for the first time. You might want to take a notebook and observe yourself and your surroundings. Don't be too concerned with technique, but try to be conscious of what's easy and what's hard. If you feel like it, practice the hard stuff. Don't feel bad about falling, walking or getting tired. Mountain biking is hard! That's part of the fun.

DAY 38

Go for a ride with a more experienced riding buddy. Following a better rider is the quickest way to build skills. Watch and learn.

DAY 40

Time to accessorize. Visit your local bike shop. If you're really enjoying yourself, treat yourself to a pair of good bike shoes. They'll make a major difference in your pedaling efficiency because they have stiff, energy-efficient soles. Also pick up a repair book if you haven't already.

DAY 43 (WEEKEND)

Ride the local. Don't be shy about talking to other riders you meet—and making riding plans with them.

DAY 45

You're beat after a long day's work. Build your energy by riding the bike path that may have seemed so daunting on Day 22—less than three weeks ago. It's easy now.

DAY 46

Join your local mountain bike club—to keep trails open, hook up with other bikers and learn repair and maintenance skills. If you don't know where to find a club, ask at the bike shop.

DAY 47

Time to check your bike to make sure everything's okay. Are both wheels on securely? Do the tires have enough air? Are the brake levers bottoming out from cable stretch? Is the shifting still smooth and quiet? Bounce the bike to listen for rattles and loose parts. If you have any questions—or questionable items—take the bike back to the shop. Otherwise, keep riding. Your 30-day checkup's just days away.

DAY 50 (WEEKEND)

Take a big ride. You can do 15 to 20 miles. Pick a trail that's relatively easy or do your local twice. Don't pick a trail that's listed as advanced. The idea is to stretch yourself a little bit. Remember, you're more likely to have a breakdown on a long ride. Make sure you can fix a flat. Carry a small repair manual—several pocket-size editions are available at bookstores and bike shops.

DAY 51

Rent a good movie. During the rest of the week, take a few small rides. Got time after work? Back to your local.

DAY 52

Take your bike to the bike shop and get the free 30-day checkup. Your cables, bearings, spokes, nuts and bolts have probably stretched or loosened during this first month of riding. You might have to leave it overnight.

DAY 57 (WEEKEND)

Feeling ambitious? This Sunday, ask your pals at the bike shop (or new pals you've met on the trail) where the hardest hill in the area is. Then ride it. It might be long, it might be short. The idea is to take it slowly and easily—but not give up. This means spinning in low gear, resting when you need to and quitting when you feel you really, really can't go anymore. Practice different body positions— and look for one that keeps both wheels on the ground without losing traction.

DAY 60

By now, you're probably riding two or three times a week. You've probably gotten your first flat. You've probably learned how to adjust your gears. In other words, you have a routine. Pat yourself on the back—and remind yourself not to become a slave to the wonderful sport you've enjoyed.

DAY 61

Ride your local after work. Take notice of your improvement.

DAY 63 (WEEKEND)

If you're in the "fearless" mode, today's the day to skip your local and try descending. Have a friend drop you off at the top of a big hill or mountain. Wear extra protective gear—jeans and a jacket if the hill's really big. But remember: Descending is dangerous. You can get seriously injured if the trail's really hairy, if you screw up or if your bike breaks.

Control the variables and control your speed. Suspension helps. As you go downhill, stay loose and comfortable. Keep your arms and legs bent to absorb bumps. If you wipe out, try to keep your body relaxed as you hurtle through the air. When you get to the bottom, smile like an idiot.

DAY 70 (WEEKEND)

Today's skill of the day is singletrack. Narrow, twisty, challenging trails are the very essence of mountain biking. You can't have more fun—or be more challenged—than when you're on singletrack. Unfortunately, riders are banned from singletrack in many places. This is because riders can spook horses and hikers if they're not careful and considerate, and because of prejudices against mountain bikers by old-guard hiking types. If there is legal singletrack in your area, find it and spend the day in ecstasy. If there isn't, ride your local. If your local is singletrack, consider yourself a lucky dog.

DAY 71

To keep singletrack—and other trails—open to riders, consider becoming a member of the IMBA. Write to IMBA, Box 7578, Boulder, CO 80306.

DAY 73

Pavement? Absolutely. Pump your tires up full and ride home from work today (get a ride there or leave your car and get a ride tomorrow). Bike commuting can be tough—you need to find shower and storage facilities—but an occasional two-wheeled jaunt home should be manageable.

DAY 76

Spend the day with your significant other, who by now has either bought a bike or is feeling very, very neglected.

DAY 77 (WEEKEND)

Join the mob. Riding solo is beautiful, magical, intense. Riding with a group is fast, competitive, frenzied. Both are a blast—but only group riding forces you to improve quickly. Why? Because trying to keep up with folks who are faster than you forces you to ride faster.

DAY 80

Here are some options: Continue your low-key riding, gradually increasing—if you wish—the frequency or difficulty of your rides. Try a race or two. Local races are a great way to meet fellow riders and test your skills. Beginner-class races are usually intense, but short.

For more information on racing, contact your local bike shop or the National Off-Road Bicycle Association. What's our favorite summertime plan? A little more riding, a race or two, topped off by a weeklong bike vacation. You can take your bike to a ski resort (such as California's Mammoth Mountain), a bike center (such as West Virginia's Elk River Touring Center) or on an organized tour. At this point you're good enough to ignore any or all of this advice: If you just want to have fun your own way, feel free.

DAY 82

Time to learn how to tune your own bike. Your repair guide will have complete information. Put a new chain on, replace your tires with higher-quality folding tires (your bike will ride better and weigh less) and check all moving parts of your bike for damage, wear and proper lubrication. Luxury option: Let the bike shop do this for you.

DAY 84 (WEEKEND)

Ride the local. If nobody's around, yodel loudly.

DAY 86

IMBA recommends that every off-road rider spend 20 hours per year—that's four or five days—doing trail maintenance. It's a great idea, and great fun. Contact your local club to find out when trail days are scheduled.

DAY 91 (WEEKEND)

Skills update: nature time. You're now an intermediate mountain biker, ready to take on any trail. That means it's time to stop awhile and appreciate nature. Today's ride is a slow one. Bring a pair of binoculars and observe the animals and plants around you. You don't have to identify them or treat it like a boring science lesson.

Just let yourself appreciate how wonderful a tool your new bike is for bringing you into nature.

DAY 98

Hey, you're good enough to decide for yourself. Go for an epic ride. Go downhilling. Whatever you want—you can do it.

DAY 100

Ask a beginner to ride with you this weekend. Go slow and be gentle. Remember, this may have been you just three months ago.

TOOLS FOR THE TRAIL ④

By Captain Dondo

Nothing ruins a ride more than a mechanical failure that forces you to walk. Sometimes a bike is so badly mangled that trailside repair is impossible. But more often, you have to hoof for one of these reasons.

1. You don't know how to do the repair.
2. You don't have the tools.
3. You don't have the parts.

This chapter tells you what to carry to eliminate reasons 2 and 3.

WHAT YOU NEED

My bag of trail tricks has been honed to a fine balance between minimalism and pragmatism. These items are all you need for fixing the most common mechanical maladies—no more, but also no less (so don't leave anything out).

Chain-rivet tool. Without one there's little hope of removing damaged links, reconnecting a broken chain or shortening it for a single-speed ride home after mangling a rear derailleur. I started carrying a chain tool the year I shredded six rear derailleurs. Those of you riding Hyperglide chains need a Hyperglide rivet tool and several spare replacement rivets.

Six-in-one tool. Mine is made by Cannondale and has 3mm, 4mm, 5mm and 6mm Allen wrenches, a flat-blade screwdriver and a Phillips screwdriver. The tools fit every Allen-head bolt and adjustment screw on my bike and fold like pocketknife blades into a compact case. The Cool Tool includes a chain-rivet tool, adjustable wrench and 14mm crank bolt socket in addition to Allen keys and

Clockwise from right: tool bag, tube, liquid lubricant, duct tape, patch kit, six-inch wrench, crankarm wrench, chain-rivet tool, six-in-one tool, tire levers.

screwdrivers. I'd really like one for Christmas.

Crankarm wrench. If you don't carry one, someday you may be stopping every quarter-mile to hammer a loose crankarm with a hunk of wood. That's not good for your sanity or your crank. These wrenches are available for 14mm, 15mm and 16mm bolts; Park makes a model with all three sizes. Some cranks, such as Campagnolo, use an Allen-head bolt. Buy the type and size that fits your crankset.

Tire levers. Mountain bike tires are pretty easy to remove with just your hands, but carrying two lightweight nylon tire levers is good insurance against the occasional tight fit.

Six-inch adjustable wrench. One size wrench fits nearly all bike nuts and bolts and straightens bent rear derailleur hangers and twisted pedal cages.

Duct tape. This is the high-tech answer to bailing wire. Roll duct tape around a pencil until you have an inch diameter, then cut it and fold a quarter-inch onto itself so you can easily find the end. Break the protruding pencil and you have a compact package of fix-it magic for booting ripped tires, mending cracked racks, splinting broken handlebars and frame tubes or immobilizing fractured bones.

Spare tube. Punctures are patchable, but valve-stem damage and major ruptures require tube replacement. Murphy's Backcountry Law dictates that you'll probably suffer one more tube demolition per ride than you have replacement tubes. So always try to fool Mr. Murphy by disguising your spare as a raisin bagel. And be sure to segregate it from your tools, which love to nibble holes. Put it in a separate pack pocket or a small nylon stuff sack.

Patch kit. Murphy's Mountain Bike Corollary guarantees that after you've replaced a blown tube, you'll ride over a thornbush. Add a couple of two-inch-square pieces of canvas or junk-tire sidewall to the supplies in your regulation bike-store kit. Then you can patch tire casing tears.

Liquid lubricant. Applying a bit of lube to your chain and derailleur pulleys will quell those maddening mid-ride squeaks from hell. It might sound frivolous—until you've endured this chirping for several hours.

Tool bag. You'll need something in which to carry all this stuff. A saddle pack keeps tools together and on your bike so you don't need to look for them before every ride. A fanny pack lets you take the tools with you when your bike is locked and unattended.

Pump (at right). Gimmicks such as carbon dioxide (CO_2) cartridges and pumps that transform into espresso makers are great, but make sure that the one you carry will actually inflate your tires. Schrader valves, the type most often found on mountain bikes, are the same as the valves on car tires. Skinnier, European-style presta valves are rarer. Some bike pumps come with a reversible head that works on either type.

EXPANDED KIT

Consider adding these items when you're embarking on multiday adventures. Or better yet, divide them among the riders in your group.

Rear brake and derailleur cables. Rear cables can always be pressed into front service, but not vice versa. So only carry rears.

Spokes. If your derailleur or chain gets caught in the rear wheel, the worst damage usually occurs to the nine outermost spokes.

Cassette cracker. In order to replace rear spokes, you'll need this tool to remove the cogs from a pre-Hyperglide cassette hub or freewheel.

Hypercracker. This is for removing the locking nut on Hyperglide and Campagnolo cassettes.

Folding tire. Expensive, yes, but Kevlar-bead tires fold into a tight bundle for easy storage. A three-inch sidewall gash 100 miles from civilization convinced me of the value.

⅛-inch freewheel bearings. Retainer rings love to unscrew in the middle of nowhere and liberate bearings. A freewheel will work without bearings, but it works better with them.

Rear derailleur. So easy to demolish, so hard to do without.

Pedal cage and rack bolts. Duct tape is great, but spare bolts are better.

Toe strap. Use it as a toe strap, tie-down, tourniquet or cuff guard. Or cut it up and eat it as an alternative to cannibalism (leather type only) when you're really lost.

RIDING RESPONSIBLY ⑤

By Hank Barlow

Riding with minimal impact is the ultimate skill in mountain biking. It's more difficult than conquering the gnarliest hill, harder than riding the Colorado Trail, more challenging than descending from the White Mountains over rocks and creeks. Why? Because focusing on the path before us is a snap compared with developing sensitivity to the ripples that our passages cause.

Put me on a rock-strewn trail twisting through a stand of spruce high in the Colorado Rockies, and my attention is guaranteed to be sharp. If it's not, I won't be able to ride. But this also creates tunnel vision. I see only the trail before me. If I encounter hikers or horseback riders, I may not notice them until the last moment. Then I'll grudgingly yield the trail or, if they pull off, ride past with a nod and a hello while my irritation at the interruption hangs in my wake like dust.

Or, if the wind has blown a tree across the trail, I'll look for a way to ride around so my rhythm is only disturbed, not broken. In my dogged pursuit of a day's pleasures, I think nothing of creating a new trail. But if I were in tune with the world around me, I would stop and carry my bike over or even take out my folding saw. Either choice would preserve the existing trail.

SETTING AN EXAMPLE

I see shortcuts all the time. In the desert, people ride across fragile cryptogamic soil just to get from one rock fin to another rather than look for a less damaging way around. They lock their rear brakes on descents and leave black streaks down the rock. In the mountains, they ride across delicate tundra for a better look at something that caught their eye, oblivious to the fact that their tracks will last for years. Worse, others may see them and blindly follow, creating a permanent scar.

Clean riding means leaving the environment the way we found it (or even better, collecting trash and removing trail-blocking trees). It also means not disrupting the experience of others we encounter, such as hikers and horseback riders. If we conduct ourselves in a responsible, caring, respectful manner, what they do in return is their responsibility. If they've developed a negative attitude toward bikers, then our politeness may make them think again. It's worth a try.

Ultimately, environmentalism is an attitude derived from our individual histories. This makes it hard to change negative dispositions. But it's also true that those responsible for harmful actions may not even be aware of them.

One thing that aggravates me is the way smokers throw down cigarette butts and burned matches. Those filter tips seem to last forever. I don't care if other people smoke; that's their business. But I do resent smokers making the earth their ashtray, not to mention the risk of starting a fire.

Mountain bikers are guilty of such actions, too. Our equivalents to filters are the foil and plastic that enclose every tube patch. When we flat we're usually a bit upset about it. Our ride has been interrupted, our rhythm shattered. If our partners stop to wait, we feel pressed to make the repair as quickly as possible. In our haste and frustration the packaging is tossed aside. When we have an awareness of the ripples that our actions create, we won't toss aside our trash.

Banana peels, apple cores and orange rinds fall into the same category but with one major difference: They degrade. However, this doesn't occur quickly (and may even take years in the desert). Meanwhile, they sit for all who follow to gaze upon. Food remains, like patch packaging, are trash and should be carried out. Leaving them behind in the wilderness is in the same philosophical realm as jabbing a cigarette butt into a van Gogh painting.

Then there are the carbon dioxide (CO_2) cartridges that have become so popular for inflating tires. I've yet to find a spent one on the trail, but they are still environmentally unsound. They add CO_2 to an atmosphere that has more than enough already, and they're simply one more unnecessary product from our throwaway society. In comparison, a hand pump can be used repeatedly and will last for years. Cartridges are like fast-food packaging: instant waste.

Tire tubes are another consideration. People seem to think that a repaired tube can't be trusted. Oh, the tire might be okay with one or two patches, but more than that and it's time to throw the thing away. But I've seen tubes with a dozen patches hold air beautifully. They won't leak unless the patches were applied improperly. We go through tires quickly enough without also trashing perfectly good tubes each time.

THE CLEAN BRAKE

One of the most obvious examples of environmentally unsound riding occurs when rear tires are skidded on descents. This can destroy trails. First a groove is worn, then rainwater rushes through and accelerates erosion. As the groove becomes deeper, riding (or even walking) inside it becomes more difficult. So you ride beside it, a new trail forms and the erosion process is repeated. Of course, on a steep hillside, there may not even be this option, and the passage can be lost.

There is no need to skid, and in fact, a sliding tire does not slow a bike more effectively. If the back wheel accidentally locks, lighten pressure on that brake while applying more to the front. This will give you far more control of your speed and direction, plus you won't be screwing up the trail for others—including yourself the next time you ride it. In addition, a skidding tire wears out faster, thus contributing to the world's trash because you have to replace it sooner. If you can't ride down without locking the rear wheel, get off and walk. Try the trail again when your descending skill has improved.

One of mountain biking's major bugaboos is mud. It can, depending on soil type, clog a bike to the point where it's unridable. Although mud can be a wonderful challenge—and it never fails to make us feel like kids—riding wet trails will gash them. Where your route crosses boggy ground and there's no way around, get friends to help you build a raised path. If the bog is seasonal, don't ride the trail until the mud has dried. If there's doubt about the effect that riding through will have, get off and carry your bike around.

Even if you don't care about preserving the environment, consider all this an opportunity to enhance your riding skills. As I said, passing cleanly through the backcountry is the greatest challenge of all. If you don't believe me, try to ride with such minimal impact that anyone following will be unable to tell you were there. You'll be amazed at how difficult it is.

How to Have a Successful
Off-Road Roadtrip

TRAVELING WITH YOUR BIKE ⑥

By Bill Strickland

Some of the cycling sages I hang with say that one reason the bicycle is humankind's most marvelous machine is that it's more than a toy and more than an exercise apparatus. It's also a vehicle. Unlike Nintendo or Nautilus, a mountain bike can take you places.

True enough. But I think it's just as important to remember that you can take your bike places, too. Your bike should be like your dog. You should feel bad when you leave it at home while you disappear for several days.

I'm no Marco Polo, but since I began mountain biking I have managed to escape my Pennsylvania base to ride in Colorado, Vermont, West Virginia, New York, Washington and even unlikely places such as Rhode Island and Indiana.

And I've never had a terrible time. I guess when you're new at it, even the lousy trips are fun. But I have made plenty of blunders that I'd rather have avoided. Maybe what I learned can help you make sure your knobby vacations don't go flat.

FAT TRAVELS

These six tips aren't everything you need to seek happy trails. They probably aren't even the most important things. (Who can decide something like that?) But I wish I'd known them sooner.

1. If you can't ride your own bike, ride your own contact points. There are both philosophical and practical reasons for taking your bike on trips rather than renting or borrowing one. In addition to the human-to-machine bonding that a shared epic ride inspires, you'll simply ride better and more comfortably on your own rig.

But if you can't take your bike—and a lot of times it isn't a practical option—you can make a loaner ride more like your own. Much of what we perceive as the feel of our bikes comes from the only three places that we actually touch it: the saddle, the pedals and the handlebar.

Two of the three are easy to transfer. Stuff your saddle and pedals into your knapsack, then stick 'em on the impostor. You'll be less likely to suffer saddle sores, knee twinges caused by unfamiliar pedal/shoe systems and other ailments.

The handlebar is tougher. You could swap grips, but even that can be a hassle. A good compromise is to try to find a scoot with the same shifting and braking system you use.

2. Ride carefully at first . . . If you try to push the envelope immediately, you'll just get frustrated. The reason is more profound than not knowing the trails.

On unfamiliar trails close to home, I can still sometimes turn in a virtuoso performance because I know the character of Pennsylvania singletrack. Ride a region long enough, and you can somewhat sense things such as how long climbs will be, how big drop-offs are or when rock patches will leap from behind blind turns. Entering a new type of terrain is like visiting a foreign culture. You should learn the tribal customs before you dance.

You might also get hurt if you try too hard. Even if you're not afraid of pain, an injury can ruin your vacation. I never thought about this until I tore my rotator cuff and put a hairline fracture in my collarbone on the penultimate day of an excursion in the Pacific Northwest. If it had happened earlier, I'd have sat by the pool for a week nursing my shoulder and a beer instead of surfing some of the best singletrack I've ever ridden.

3. . . . But not too carefully. Mountain biking isn't needlepoint (my advance apologies to the various stitching proponents and activists). Part of the fun is breaking the pattern. I've noticed a kind of theory of relativity on my trips. The closer I get to the end, the wilder I ride because there's less lost time at risk. Scare yourself a little. You'll be better for it.

4. Take this stuff. Hey, this isn't "Hints from Heloise." Instead of following one of those goofball packing lists, just remember these guidelines.

- You need twice as many socks and inner tubes as you think.
- You do need an extra pair of shoes and gloves.
- Arm warmers double your supply of jerseys.
- Don't pack your helmet in soft-sided, checked baggage. I

know a guy whose brand new Terramoto was mauled by baggage gorillas.

⦿ If you're going to interact with real people, wear duds that look like real clothes. You won't appreciate the wisdom of this until you stumble into a redneck bar wearing tights. I especially like the Large Hardwear gear and Cannondale ATW shirts and shorts that you can pull over your cycling attire.

5. Go somewhere different. If, like me, you're an eastern-style pick-and-poke rider, plan a vacation on super-fast buff (smooth) stuff. Go to the big altitude if you're a flatlander. And if you're one of those gifted souls who lives in a mountain bike mecca, explore the singletrack in a place like Alabama (which, by the way, I hear is first-rate in spots).

Scenery changes are good for the psyche, but they also feed the skill monster. In five days in Colorado, I learned to ride switchbacks. A week in West Virginia taught me about wet-root riding. And on torturous climbs in Vermont, I learned how to realistically fake mechanical difficulties when I got tired.

Travel will make you a complete rider. But at the same time . . .

6. Don't wait for the big trips. Haul your bike with you whenever possible. I'll admit that my mid-winter trip to Indiana was a mountain biking bust. But my two-wheeler did get me out of a crowded in-law holiday house and into a snow-covered ghost of a cornfield on a sunny morning. It was cool, sort of.

I try to take my bike on any trip that involves an overnight stay. You never know what you'll find at the other end of an itinerary, and I'm still new enough at mountain biking that an impromptu ride in a tiny forest in another state feels like big adventure to me. Maybe one day I'll be experienced enough to scoff. But I hope not.

CRASH COURSE ⑦

By Bob Howells

e've seen the ads, the videos, the magazine photos: gnarly mountain bikers grinding through impossible terrain, catching air, slicing around corners in clouds of dust, bunny-hopping boulders, doing wheelies through streams. We've grimaced and chuckled simultaneously at face plants, endos, biffs and crash-landings. But we always see the poor schmo who goes down get up and dust himself off. Either that, or the camera turns away . . . .

The subliminal message is easy to translate: Mountain bikes possess the invincibility of army tanks, and the occasional mishap has the inconsequential effect of cartoon violence. The pictures never show mountain bikers being airlifted to an emergency room. They don't show fractures, peeled-away skin or surgeries being performed. They don't portray anything that hints at real pain.

Sure, most of us would acknowledge, if pressed, that mountain biking can be dangerous. But most of us would admit, if honest, that we get a charge from flouting danger. And surely we're influenced to some extent by those subliminal messages. Somewhere, some insidiously influenced synapse triggers a mandate to the hapless body: "Go for it. You can make it."

I have my own experience with that syndrome. In nine years of mountain biking, I'd fallen only on slow-speed technical stuff. But not long ago I took a steep, rocky trail way too fast, got launched by an invisible mound at the bottom and fractured my pelvis at both hip joints.

After surgery, two weeks in the hospital, a lot of pain, two months in a wheelchair and two months of physical therapy, I'm riding—very carefully—again. An isolated instance? Maybe. But I know four other mountain bikers who have suffered fractured pelvises—three of them, like me, in the hip joint. I feel that my caution is justified.

A GROWING TREND

No national statistics on mountain bike injuries are available. We intuitively know that the severity of the injuries doesn't compare with road riding. Free of cars and other street perils, we mountain bikers are comparatively safe. And the bikes are incredible. These days we even have suspension to insulate us from the bumps of the trail. Most of us strap on helmets, straddle our sturdy frames, pedal off aboard strong wheels, knobby tires and suspension forks and assume, to some degree, a sense of security.

But people do get hurt. Hospital emergency rooms near mountain bike hotbeds confirm that mountain bike injuries are on the rise in proportions matching the rapid growth of the sport. The emergency room at Allen Memorial Hospital in Moab, Utah, treats 10 to 30 mountain bikers on a typical spring or fall weekend. That's 5 to 15 hospitalized riders a day! In fact, according to physician's assistant April Randle, mountain bike injuries account for a recent doubling of cases in the small-town emergency room, and the hospital has built an addition to accommodate the increased volume.

ERs in other mountain meccas such as Durango and Gunnison (near Crested Butte), Colorado, and Mount Snow, Vermont, all report a similar pattern of mountain bike injuries. Dirt rash—the painful scraping off of the epidermis—tops the list. Broken collarbones, the frequent result of an unscheduled trip over the handlebar, are second, followed by wrist fractures and ankle injuries. Hip and pelvic fractures are rarer, but hospitals in each of the areas mentioned have treated a few.

Notice what's missing from this list? At least in the mountain biking hotbeds, where most riders wear helmets, head injuries are rare. And most of those are reported to be mild concussions.

Fortunately, mountain biking deaths of any cause are extremely rare. Jim Hasenauer, president of the International Mountain Bicycling Association, says he knows of eight mountain bike–related deaths since the bikes were first mass-produced in 1983. Two of those were equestrians whose mounts were spooked by mountain bikers. The mountain bikers who have died typically were unable to make a high-speed turn in steep terrain and fell a great distance to their death.

RIDING WITH GRACE

Unlike road-riding deaths and injuries, which are often caused by cars and other unavoidable hazards, the vast majority of mountain biking injuries are entirely preventable. Competent riders on well-maintained bikes who ride within their skill level are virtually in charge of their environments. They're safe. But how do you develop the skills and the consciousness to become such a rider?

You can try a skills clinic or the tips we provide, but a big part of it is simply knowing yourself. After all, lack of skill and experience can get a novice hurt, but many seasoned riders also crash. What's to blame? Safety experts say that it's ego and competitiveness. And it's precisely those traits that prevent many riders from ever learning safe riding techniques in the first place.

I'm among the ranks of those who won't hesitate to get off and walk, but it took a catastrophe to make me a safe rider. And I thought I was a safe rider before. I agree with Hasenauer when he says, "Part of the joy of mountain biking is the thrill." And speed is unquestionably the main component of the thrill. But a safe rider is acutely aware of his limits, uninfluenced by gonzo images or even riding companions. He builds his skills as gradually and gracefully as a dancer.

I like the dance analogy, because somehow riding a mountain bike reminds me of a great ballet dancer soaring into the air. What I really marvel at is not the height that the dancer reaches, but the way he touches down so lightly and gracefully continues the dance.

WAYS TO REDUCE YOUR RISK

If you want to ride safely, follow these tips.

Know your limits. Ride within them. Never be reluctant to walk any stretch of trail—downhill or uphill—that you feel might be beyond your skill level. Don't be swayed by personal bravado, friends or the subliminal implication fostered by advertisements that you can do anything on a mountain bike.

Be especially careful on unfamiliar trails. Remember, professionals always ride a race course at least once at less than full speed before "going for it."

Look out for others. Warn hikers of your approach (call out "cyclist approaching") and slow to walking pace as you pass. Yield to horseback riders.

Covet grace and finesse above speed. That way, you'll be in full control when you do go fast.

Allow plenty of distance. This applies to the distance between you and the rider ahead. The rule of thumb is at least one foot of space for each mile per hour of speed.

Don't ride alone. When you're in desolate country, always ride with a buddy and always tell someone where you're going. Both are easy ways to prevent a broken leg from becoming a death by hypothermia, dehydration or worse.

Develop your skills gradually. Attempting a quantum leap in your abilities may result in a crash landing. Six-time NORBA national champion and pro mountain bike racer and coach Ned Overend advises: "Build your abilities before you build your speed."

Part 2 Basic Riding

Skills

LOOKING AHEAD ⑧

By Bill Strickland

I got my eyes today—my mountain biking eyes. And man, do things ever look bright.

There I was, about midway up one of my regular hill pushes—past the wide beginning slope and into the section where the steep sides funnel you and pebbles and rocks and leaves and branches and animal bones and everything else that's ever fallen within ten feet of the trail into the center of the singletrack so that it's even harder to negotiate than this sentence. Unless you're on your feet, of course. Like me.

But the local cycling shamans were still on their wheels. Up ahead, the last of them was spinning through the final and toughest

Bill suffers from no anticipation....
CREEK!
LOG!
Yiiieeee!!
ROCKS!

part of the climb. Rocks jut from the incline like fossilized dinosaur teeth. Get past that jagged jawbone of a path, and you have to slow to a near standstill, pivot right and butter yourself through a turn so tight it'll take hair off your arms.

I'm not a horrible mountain biker—about average. But as I watched the last rider thread the trail that I'd never ridden successfully, I knew that something was missing—something beyond experience or handling tricks. The mountain biker above me was using simple moves, stuff I could do. The difference between us? He was pedaling. I was pushing.

What I lacked was deep and basic, like a flaw in my fat-tire foundation that skewed everything above. I'd always known this hole existed but never knew what to fill it with.

Reminded me of chess. Swear on a stack of Ground Controls, that's what I thought of right at that moment.

I used to love the game. Wasn't too bad, either. Which also means I wasn't too good. About average. I still mess around with a board once in a while, but for the most part I quit when I realized I'd never be competitive because I didn't have chess vision.

The true masters focus on how they want the game to end or on the crucial midgame move that will decide the outcome, and play backward from there. There's no hesitation. They know where they're going. Every move is sure—and those moves that appear to be mistakes are really just sacrifices to set up victory.

Guys like me might play only two or three moves ahead. Beginners are even worse, playing for the best position move by move. Or, I thought as I dropped my bike and concentrated on the true master finishing his two-wheeled dance up the incline, we ride move by move.

FROM ROOK TO KING

Only certain geniuses are lucky enough to be born with chess vision. But anyone can acquire off-road vision and start riding a little bit more like a master instead of a move-by-move hacker. Off-road vision is accessible because it's not abstract (the trail is real and right there in front of you) and because you gain this new view in small, easily learned steps. Here they are.

Don't stare at what you want to miss. Your bike follows your eyes. Fixate on that four-foot drop-off and you'll be in it. Instead, scan for obstacles and focus on them just until they register in your brain. Then turn your sight to where you want to go. Trust that organic computer of yours to plot a clear course.

This doesn't mean that you should never focus. Don't become a

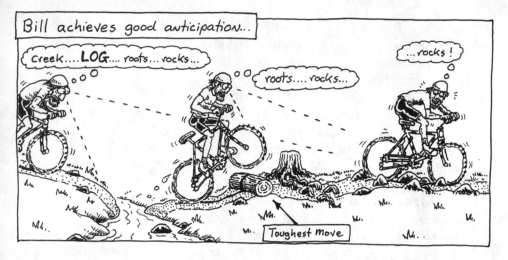

blind battering ram. Need to backspin so your pedal clears a rock? Have to thread your wheel between two logs? Look at these and other problem areas, but remember to concentrate on the good line (the cleanest route past an obstacle).

Don't look at your wheel. By then, it's too late to react to trail conditions. Give yourself lead time by focusing farther out. Most mountain bikers cite 30 to 40 feet as a typical distance. But novices are usually more comfortable beginning at half that and gradually expanding. Don't forget to adjust, either. In slow, technical sections, I focus only a single bike length ahead. On fast, smooth descents, I've previewed up to 100 feet.

Want proof that this 30-feet concept will improve your off-road riding? Try it with other parts of your life. I've done so while driving (we all think we look far enough ahead, but concentrate and you'll be surprised how often you're looking just past the hood), jogging, even walking through the house. It improves everything except reading and using the bathroom.

Scope everything. Pay attention to more than just the obvious obstacles. Will the trail surface affect you? If the trail cuts sideways on an incline, is it angled into the hill or away? Glance away from the trail. Do you have room to biff or do you need to watch those trees on the right? Will that parallel stream cross the singletrack around the next turn? All this helps you decide on the best line.

Pick out the "peak" move. Finally, identify the section that will require the most skill or power or both to clean (get across without putting a foot down). Plot your line backward from there.

I used to plot forward and hope for the best. ("Whew, got over that. Next, look at that log. Hey, where'd that turn come from . . . .") Now, almost every section of trail seems to order itself into one big challenge that's preceded by a series of five to seven small obstacles that I know I can clean without much thought.

I arrive at that big move in better position because, like the chess champ, I know my ultimate goal and can make sacrifices to set myself up for success.

My old goal was to find the smoothest line move by move. Now I ride the line that gives me the best chance of cleaning the final move at the end. Sometimes this means that instead of, say, skirting the two logs before the peak move—a wheelie over an eight-inch tree trunk—I bump over them. But the additional bumps let me ride straight over the trunk instead of at the tricky angle that the "smooth and easy" line would have put me on.

I used to think of lines as smooth or bumpy. Now it's just good (on the bike) or bad (pushing).

PRACTICE, PRACTICE

I worked on one step each week and needed another few weeks to put it all together in even the roughest fashion. The following drills helped.

Stop. Glance at the next 30 feet of trail, then close your eyes. Pick your way clean in your imagination, then open your eyes and see how well you plotted your course. You might discover that you consistently neglect to notice one type of terrain feature (a sideways slope or loose dirt, for instance). Fight this mental block.

Go against advice. Try looking directly at what you want to miss and see if you still can miss it. Look only at the ground in front of your wheel and see how much harder riding is. I don't know why these "aversion therapies" work, but they somehow sharpen the skills you're purposely neglecting.

Take the wrong line. Or try a line you've never considered. Or veer from the tracks of the good riders in front of you. But keep your focus on the peak move and still build your small moves toward it. Your failures will teach you a lot about what makes a good line.

But your successes, which will be more numerous than you'd think, will show you that finding the perfect line over the small stuff isn't the point. Setting up for the peak move is.

Finally, ask a really good rider about all this. If the answer isn't a blank stare, it will be a statement such as "I guess I do that, but I don't really pay attention."

Ah, light at the end of the singletrack. That rider's mountain biking vision was once slow and clumsy. But once he opened his off-road eyes, he never had to think about them again.

GOING OVER OBSTACLES ⑨

By Bill Strickland

Must've had mud in my ear. When the local dirt dudes dropped by this morning, I thought they asked me to go mountain biking. But they obviously meant mountain hiking because that's how I spent most of my time.

The trail was rooted, rutted and littered with branches, rocks and entire trees that through some miracle of mountain biking physics all managed to fall in such a way that completely blocked the single-track.

The experienced riders had bikes that blasted over it all like metal mountain cats. My machine is more like that survivor in airplane-crash movies who breaks his leg and has to be shoved, slung, toted and tossed to safety.

What was most discouraging was that just about every obstacle was less than six inches high. Anything bigger was so much beyond my ability that I didn't feel bad abandoning wheels for heels. But this little stuff doesn't require pyrotechniques. All you gotta do is roll over it.

The last time I tried, the bike slammed to a stop while I continued forward and banged my belly into the stem. The time before that, the front wheel whipped sideways and pitched me off the trail. I got half the bike over once, but hung up the back wheel. Whenever I get farther than that, the rear wheel rebounds off the obstacle and tosses me over the handlebar.

I was ready to quit, leave my bike for dead and save myself. But just as I made that decision, one of the fat-tire wizards dropped back and gave me some magic advice that turned my disaster movie into a rip-roaring, action-adventure, feel-good flick.

WHAT THE SHAMAN SAID

He explained the five basic steps for scaling small obstacles. Within 15 minutes of practicing them, I began rolling over previously unridable stuff. And in the week since, I've cleared almost every blockade smaller than six inches, sometimes even nailing things up to eight inches.

Pay attention to your mistakes. They're your keys to success. Each type of crash I had was related to one of these five steps. You'll see, for instance, that if your front wheel clears but you leave a layer of your face lying on the trail, you need to work on step 4.

1. Make sure you have enough speed. This keeps your front wheel from stopping when it hits, helps prevent it from turning sideways and is vital to getting the entire bike over.

Maintaining forward motion mostly depends on approaching the object quickly enough. I rarely did, until my mud mentor told me to approach with enough speed so that even if I didn't pedal for two feet before the collision, I'd still clear the obstacle. This will seem way fast at first, but give it a try.

I also learned to let go of the brakes. I had almost always kept two fingers on the levers, just for security, I guess. But I'd often panic in

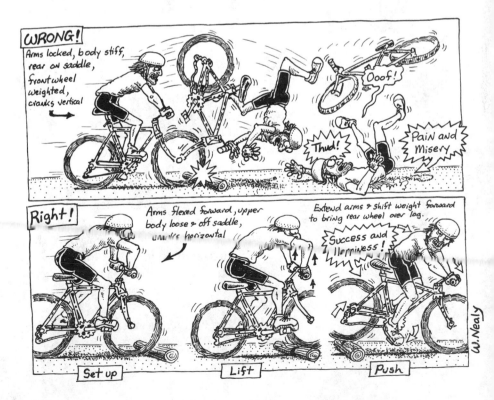

mid-rollover and brake. I'll probably return to two-fingered just-in-case readiness some day, but until I break the habit of premature halts, I'm moving my fingers from the brake levers to the handlebar before every attempt.

2. Assume the position. This makes the rest of the process possible. The "ready" position is shown in the illustration (see page 43): both legs bent equally, crankarms parallel to the ground, butt slightly off the saddle, elbows and knees not locked. This basic technique will be useful for other stunts as your experience grows. Practice it.

3. Unweight the front wheel while holding it steady. This prevents the belly bang and the sideways-wheel twitch. To unweight, shift your body slightly rearward from the ready position. But not too far. A few inches is usually enough. You're doing it right when your elbows are a little more than halfway between a 90-degree bend and a straight-armed position. And keep those joints loose.

Steadiness is important, too. Imagine that you're jogging and encounter a 12-foot brick wall. It's easier to turn and run alongside it than climb. This is how your front wheel behaves. Unless you force it to "climb," it will turn. Grip the handlebar firmly and countersteer against the wheel's twitches. It'll take a while to find the compromise between unweighting the wheel and keeping control, but you'll get there.

4. Absorb the impact with your elbows and knees. Your joints are the original suspension devices. Use them right and you'll be less likely to get stuck halfway over an obstacle (and less likely to eat dirt after flying over the handlebar).

When the front wheel hits, let the bike come up toward your chest. If your elbows are loose, they'll bend as this happens. When your front wheel hits the ground on the other side, return your arms to their original position. This pushes the bike away from you (forward) and helps bring the rear wheel over.

Your knees play a similar role, but it happens more naturally than with the elbows. Stiff arms are the reason for most face plants.

5. Return to the ready position while unweighting the rear wheel. This eliminates the possibility of being thrown when the back wheel hits the obstacle. Simply shift your weight forward, returning to the original ready position. This happens naturally, except for the first few times when you're so scared that you stiffen your arms and death-grip the bar.

Clearing bigger obstacles relies on these same five steps, with some trickier elements such as wheelies and additional weight shifts thrown in.

Wheelie Gweat Ways
to Clear Obstacles

POPPING WHEELIES ⑩

By Bill Strickland

Conquering gravity is one of the essences of our sport's soul, and the wheelie is the most basic air maneuver. If you don't have this bit of mountain bikeness down deep inside, the thinking goes, all your riding will be somewhat hollow.

There must be something to this theory because wheelie failure punctures your esteem at a level usually reserved for things such as not finding mates, jobs or friends. It hurts more than it should.

You give a mighty heave on the handlebar, an involuntary grunt comes out of your mouth and—nothing. Maybe a millimeter of space opens between your front wheel and the earth. Meantime, you're out of control up top, jerking around way out of proportion to the movement below. If the neighborhood wheelies got together in the sandlot to play baseball, yours would be the last one picked. At the end of the game, they would beat your wheelie up and send it home crying.

Still, even the biggest gravity geek has an inner wheelie waiting to take off. Once it happens, all this heavy philosophical hoo-ha lifts, and you can concentrate on the purely practical benefits: With wheelies, you'll clean bigger obstacles (anything taller than six inches won't automatically put you off), you won't take a beating on smaller stuff because you're lifting your bike over most of it and your control and balance will improve. Wheelies are great for jumping over bumps on fast downhills—in effect, they remove the obstacle. Your buddies who can't wheelie will have to slow way down to stay in the saddle when they hit a bump.

It's the wheel thing: Think up, think forward projection, think success.

'SCUSE ME WHILE I KISS THE SKY

Here's how I found my first wheelie, and how I got it to grow sky-high (well, knee-high . . . but everything's relative).

Getting off the ground. The basic wheelie is incredibly simple. You approach whatever obstacle you're approaching in the "ready" position: both legs bent equally, crankarms parallel to the ground, butt slightly off the saddle and elbows and knees not locked. (By the way, this basic mountain biking stance is useful for lots of other cool moves. Get used to it.)

Unweight the front wheel by sliding back slightly. This keeps you from flipping forward when you ram the obstacle. But be sure to keep a good grip on the handlebar, or the wheel will turn when it hits.

On impact, pull the handlebar up and back (toward your chest). Your elbows should bend like you're trying to rein a horse, or as if you're pulling an oar back in the last part of a rowing stroke.

The combination of your pull and the obstacle's push will raise your front wheel. Hey, you're flying and styling. Sort of.

Getting off the ground by yourself. Yeah, that's a cheater's wheelie. But the basic feel won't change once you start popping with your own power.

To get unaided front air, press down on the handlebar before you unweight the wheel. This compresses the tire. Shift your weight back and the wheel will rebound, raising itself slightly off the ground. When this happens, row (or rein, or whatever you can think of to remember to pull the bar up and back). The wheel will rise higher. It's like combining two small wheelies into a larger one.

Another technique for gaining verticality is the power stroke. While in your easiest gear, mash the pedal down with your dominant foot just as you row. This doesn't click for me yet, but it doesn't disrupt my timing or balance, so I keep trying.

Getting back to the ground. Okay, you're three-quarters over. Now what? Shift forward, back to the "ready" position. This unweights the rear wheel so it won't hang up on the obstacle. But look out, it's easy to shift too far forward and flip over the handlebar—the classic "endo."

The solution is to find a balance point. You want to keep your body back but keep your weight off the rear wheel at the same time. I have the best luck when I try to concentrate my mass over the bottom bracket.

IT AIN'T THAT EASY

Nope. Sorry. Shedding your weeniehood involves getting cooked by the trail at least a few times. Here are five common mistakes (and solutions)

Pulling the wheelie too soon or too late. Ouch. To keep your front tire from bouncing off the obstacle, adjust your timing. If the wheel is falling on the object, begin later. If it's running into the object, start sooner.

Not compressing the wheel enough. If the first part of your two-part wheelie isn't happening, try this: Instead of trying to press down harder, press down longer.

Not shifting your weight back. In my first few attempts I squashed the front tire correctly but didn't move backward. I was trying to do all the work with my elbows. But pulling the handlebar accomplishes nada if your weight is on the front wheel.

Mistiming. If you never wheelie more than three or four inches, it's because you aren't pulling the wheel higher after the initial compression-caused jump. You're probably rowing too soon. Instead let the wheel rise to the top of its compression flight before you pull the bar.

Letting your front get your rear in trouble. I've lofted my leading wheel over foot-high obstacles. But then I've crashed and burned. Wheelie ability develops faster than the other skills needed to cross way-high stuff. Around seven inches is my rarely miss level, eight inches is safe but not sure, nine inches involves a lot of scary sounds and crunches I can't control or understand and anything bigger happens only on a good gut-check day. Or a bad common-sense day.

HOP TO IT! ⑪

By Hank Barlow

Many of you can easily lift the front wheel, but you're still having trouble getting both of them off the ground. Let's try to fix that.

If you can't hold a wheelie, don't worry about it. The point of this skill isn't the wheelie itself but simply the front-wheel lift. If you can loft it over a six-inch log, you can bunny-hop the log.

The trick for me was dropping my wrists. Until I did this, my attempts at bunny-hopping were consistently feeble. This may be your primary problem, too. Let's begin with a quick review of the entire technique.

Front-wheel lift. To loft the front wheel you need to shift weight back and pull up on the grips just as you apply a hard pedal stroke. Watch out—the wheel may come up so quickly that you tip over backwards. If so, simply moderate your effort. But if the wheel barely lifts, shift to your lowest gear and try again. Keep practicing until you can do it at will with full control.

Back-wheel lift. Next, learn to do a back-wheel wheelie. Find soft ground to practice on in case you fall. Riding slowly, simultaneously shift weight forward and apply the front brake only, then pull up with both feet (assuming you're using toe clips and straps). Practice until you can instantly lift the rear wheel several inches any time you want. Don't try to get extreme; you're just trying to learn to unweight it.

Whole-bike lift. Okay, now you're ready to bunny-hop. Put a four-inch-diameter log in your soft practice area. You'll need enough speed for the back wheel to clear the log during the time you're in the air. But before you hop, you have to do a few things: First, pivot your hands back, drop your wrists and hold on tight.

(continued on page 52)

Elements of Flight

Now let's break bunny-hopping into its components.

step 1 Flex the tires with a sudden, sharp weighting action. Do this by standing with the crankarms parallel to the ground, then jumping your weight onto the pedals.

step 2 Immediately lift the front wheel (like a plane lifting the nose wheel before the main gear follows).

step
3
Twist the grips forward as if you're trying to pivot the bike
around the handlebar. Simultaneously pull up with your feet.

step
4
Envision your bike arcing upward and forward over the log.
Here is where many riders go wrong. Instead of projecting
the bike's path, they lift straight up. This won't get you
six or seven feet ahead to the other side of the log.

Then use your bike like a springboard. Before you jump, drop your weight down hard to flex the tires. Then immediately spring up and over the log.

Confused? You won't be. Once you feel the motion, it'll all make sense. In the meantime, keep practicing these moves.

It may help to think of those times that you've flown off a diving board. Remember how you'd take three steps, and on the third step, you'd gracefully lift into the air, then land on the end with both feet. The board would bend deeply beneath your flexed legs, then spring back to help launch your flight. Your body arced through the air, landing well in front.

Basically, bunny-hopping is no different from diving off a springboard. All the same elements are there: storing energy, releasing energy, then propelling yourself up and out with a powerful leg push. Sure, a springboard has vastly more launching capacity than a bike's tires and frame, but the action is the same.

Forward projection is critical. The trick that makes bunny-hopping work for me is envisioning the bike smoothly lifting off and soaring over the obstacle, then landing on the rear wheel just before the front hits. At least that's my objective. In truth, my flights are rarely so accomplished. Usually, my rear wheel bumps over because I didn't get it high enough. Which is okay because I've passed the obstacle without dismounting, and the rear wheel was unweighted so no harm came to rim or tube. I also tend to land on my front wheel first, but, again, that's no problem if I shift my weight back in time and stay off the front brake.

But once in a while I hit a jump just right and land on both wheels so smoothly I barely even notice. This feels great! And after experiencing proper bike flight, I have a keener sense of what I should do next time. This will work for you, too. Keep trying until you nail one, then think about everything you did right. The next perfect hop will come much sooner.

An excellent method for learning the moves is to fly off small rollers. A short, fast uphill followed by a sudden drop-off will let you experience the sensations of flying and landing without having to launch yourself.

The trick when flying off bumps is to touch down with your back wheel first. This means you need to lift the front wheel. But instead of doing this in the vertical plane, project it up and forward.

Practice getting flight time at every safe opportunity. The more you're in the air, the more comfortable you'll be when you're there. Keep jumping and keep trying to picture the perfect bunny-hop. Eventually you'll get it, guaranteed.

THE LUNGE ⑫

By Bill Strickland

I love the lunge. The lunge loves me. We do fun, nonbeginnerish things together—getting over logs on uphill trails, for instance. It makes me think I won't always ride like a goof. And it can do the same for you.

The funny part is, I thought it was a mistake. It happened almost accidentally the first time, one of those instinctual moves that emerges when your brain unplugs. There's a boulder on one of my local singletrack grunts that sticks up about hub-high. I tried it three times, then filed it under "dismount and walk" (cross-referenced with "skinned knees," "technicolor bruises" and "epidermal pain").

Until one day, I'm dog-tired. I pedal up to the thing, lift my front wheel and do the lunge. It feels awkward, like a move I'm forced to make to compensate for some shortcoming in my technique. But it works. I'm up. I'm over. I'm pedaling. So I keep doing it.

A week or so later, I ask some of the certified rad guys around here about it. "Oh yeah," they say. "Great move. Real useful."

DEFYING GRAVITY

As usual, those dirt dudes were right. I just wish they'd told me sooner. Since I started refining my rough attempts at this cool move, I clean (ride without dabbing, or putting a foot down) more uphill obstacles than ever. It also works on level or downhill stuff that's tall enough to grab your chainrings. I've gotten out of ruts, gulches and holes and even scaled steep banks with the lunge.

This is a low-speed (beginner's pace) maneuver. Thrashers get over this stuff with momentum. When approaching something like an uphill log, the pro style is to accelerate, stop pedaling, unweight the front wheel and let inertia handle the situation. It takes confidence, guts and experience.

I have all three of those things. Just not in big enough quantities. So here's how I lunge over instead.

1. Lift your front wheel over the obstacle. Even if you can't do a wheelie on level ground, you can loft on an uphill. It's much easier. Press down on the handlebar to compress the front tire. Then pull up and back. To get maximum front air, combine the pulling movement with a hard pedal stroke (known as a power stroke). Then level those cranks. You don't want to catch a low one on the log.

2. Pull your body forward until you're over the front end. Your butt should be off the saddle. Your elbows should be bent. The physics—moving body on a moving bike—create something called counterforce that will slow the bike. If you didn't start with much speed, you might even come to a standstill. Don't panic.

3. Shove your bike forward. This sounds crazy and impossible and un-novice-like, but it is almost pure instinct. Almost. Your body knows you can do this but your mind doesn't. Physically, the feat is easy. You're strong enough to push your bike. (Don't you roll it beside you all the time?) But it takes some kind of conceptual click to realize that you can push your bike forward underneath you.

You might want to practice on level ground first. Slow to a walking pace, then bend your elbows until you're close to the handlebar. Shove it away from you. Now try to pull the bike back under you. Eventually, you'll sense how the bike can roll beneath your body.

Beginners think we're riveted to the center of the bike. The actual relationship is more like when the bad guy in a Western walks on top of a train. While it rolls along, he can move to the front of the car, or the back, or just stay in the center. Of course, his movements won't affect the train. He doesn't weigh enough to alter its motion. But put that same size body on a bike and see what happens.

Stick with it. Do it right once, and you'll always know how.

4. Pedal. If you kept your cranks level, you should be ready to mash out a hard stroke to get going again and pull the last bit of your rear wheel over. If your feet aren't in a position to give a good power stroke, you're making the same mistake I sometimes do.

During the lunge I might torque the right pedal down. I think my body does this to help generate more thrust. The pedal usually catches on the obstacle. Even if it doesn't, I can't generate a power stroke. So I flounder at the easiest point of the whole move—after getting over. That's almost more frustrating than not having the confidence to even attempt cleaning a tough log or rock. But only almost.

CLIMBING CLINIC ⑬

Nothing makes me feel more like a beginner than blowing a climb—especially one I should have made. I know you've been there, too. Your rear wheel suddenly decides to retract its claws and spin out instead of gripping the dirt. Or you try to roll up and over the smallest thing—a twig, an ant—but don't have enough momentum. If you're lucky, you manage to drag your bike out of the way and stand there like a doof while the real mountain bikers pass.

If you're unlucky, you sprawl across the trail and ruin the climb for everyone. Either way, it's a long walk to the top.

And I hate it. Heeling interrupts the rhythm of wheeling. Whatever we're looking for out there is harder to find on foot. I mean, how mystically fun do you think surfing would be if its disciples had to walk to the top of waves? I believe not only that what goes up must come down, but also that for maximum euphoria, you should go up on what you want to come down on. Ride it all.

That's certainly an admirable ideal. But it's also—at least from a beginner's standpoint—an impossible one. Why don't we start with "Ride more of it than you used to."? Here are three basic climbing strategies to help you do just that. They aren't flashy but they work, and they form the foundation that other ascending skills are built on. The next chapter looks at tricks and tips for climbing more quickly and more efficiently and for conquering longer, tougher, steeper and more technical inclines.

1. Ride in the climber's position. Just as there is a standard stance for descending (pedals level, weight slightly off the saddle and elbows and knees loose to absorb shock), a certain climbing position is most effective for most situations.

Flex your elbows and bend forward at the hips, keeping your back straight. You should be leaning toward the handlebar, and your butt should be pushed back on the saddle a bit. This posture lowers your center of gravity, distributes your weight between the front and rear and allows you to easily make the weight shifts and movements you'll need to maintain traction and power. (We look at those later.)

Most inexperienced climbers don't bend toward the bar enough. Rather than preventing spinout, the "way-back" position unweights the front wheel—which either causes the riders to stop or makes them lose rear traction anyway when they suddenly scoot forward to keep the front down.

If you want to go up, you have to get down. Lean. My nose is usually about 15 inches above the intersection of the stem and handlebar. Yes, I measured. (And yes, I looked silly.)

2. Maintain traction. You do this by modifying your standard position. As the pitch steepens, lean more toward the bar (drop your nose closer). This puts more weight over the front and, at the same time, pushes your butt back to keep weight over the rear tire.

Tune yourself until you find the lean angle that keeps both wheels rooted. (If the front wheel's loose: too little lean; if the back one's loose: too much.) You'll eventually learn what lean matches what pitch. At first you'll overshoot the sweet spot both ways, but don't worry. The adjustments are more subtle than you expect. Keep trying.

When the incline gets steep enough, the simple lean won't work. Keep the front wheel down by leaning waaay over—I've had my nose past the handlebar and as little as four inches above it—and by sliding forward onto the tip of the saddle. (This is one reason that pros like narrow saddles with long noses.)

But with all your weight forward, what about the back wheel? You can keep it grooved by pulling back on the handlebar. This often provides a climbing breakthrough for new riders. It makes the rear wheel dig in. In the next chapter you'll learn an even trickier move—how to "row yourself" up walls masquerading as hills.

A final note: Some suspension forks make a bike's front end taller, so you might have to lean more than your rigid friends.

3. Understand the stand. When you rise out of the saddle, you use about 12 percent more oxygen and raise your heart rate about 8 percent. Or so the lab rats say. Whatever the numbers, standing is harder on your body. It requires more effort because your legs must provide locomotion and support your weight.

But if you don't stand at least occasionally, you're climbing without one of your most valuable skills. Among other things, standing lets you deliver more power to the pedals. It can delay fatigue because it uses your muscles differently. And it lets you stretch during extended climbs.

Even so, a bad stand is worse than no stand. Here's how to make the transition without losing speed, control or traction.

As your foot comes around to begin a downstroke, shift to a harder gear (if you don't, you waste energy with choppy pedal strokes), then rise out of the saddle.

If you have bar-ends, move your hands out to them. You should be as upright as the pitch will allow, with your chest over the handlebar. Your lower back should be straight. Sway the bike from side to side (but no more than a foot each way).to establish a rhythm and make your downstrokes more direct and powerful. Some riders like to pull up on the bar to do this. I push because I can do so without clenching my hands.

You've nailed the technique when you realize why it's sometimes described as "running on the pedals." If you feel jerky and out of control, you're either not pushing a big enough gear or you're completely straightening your leg on the downstroke. Go for 95 percent straightening and concentrate on pushing and pulling through a complete circle. This will eliminate the dead spot.

As with most things mountain bike, there are no rules for how often and how long to stand—just plenty of generalizations. Here are the helpful ones: Try not to sit back down on a steep grade; you'll stall. If possible, wait till you have a break in the climbing And remember to shift back to an easy gear as you return to the saddle. Most heavy riders do better when they climb seated more than they stand. The opposite applies to light riders. If you use a suspension fork, stay in the saddle as much as possible. (The power thrusts of standing pedaling make the fork bob and wastes energy.) Most novices don't stand enough, and when they do, they stand too long.

Got it? Now go use it.

UPHILL BATTLE ⑭

By Bill Strickland

In the previous chapter I said that no off-road situation makes you feel more like a beginner than bailing a climb that everyone else makes. Believe me.

Even so, we keep mountain biking, don't we? And we aim for the crest every time. There's something noble about being a novice. Every summit matters so much to us.

Maybe this is why a hundred flubbed climbs can be erased with a single ascent in which you realize the opposite of my opening statement is also true: You never feel more like a real mountain biker than when you conquer a climb you once couldn't—or, even better, when you leave your friends scattered behind along an incline.

I've been tasting this particular glory more and more lately. I like it. I want more. Here are ten strategies that will help you gobble up tougher, longer climbs.

1. Relax. When challenged by a climb, many beginners clench in preparation and don't unclench until they crest or crash. Much of this stems from anxiety. ("How much of a boob will I look like this time?") But I also believe that some newcomers think—thanks to the mass-media stereotype of the swelled-muscle shredhead bashing his bike up a hill—that we're supposed to climb that way.

Don't. Stay loose and you'll save energy, absorb more shock and be less likely to lose control when rolling over loose sections or obstacles.

On smooth, not-too-steep ascents, I climb like a roadie, with a relaxed upper body and soft hands. Keep an easy hold on the grips or bar-ends. Drum your fingers to keep them loose. Your jaw and hands are good indicators. If they're tight, your shoulders and upper body probably are, too.

2. Spin when you can. It kills me when one of those fitness gods breezes past me and blithely recommends that I maintain 90 rpm—as if the problem is that I'm simply forgetting to count my pedal strokes. Don't they ride with real people? Or am I the only mountain biker on earth so unfit that I sometimes climb at 1 rpm in the granny gear? (Well, that's what it feels like, anyway.)

Nonetheless, it's good to spin when you can. If you have the gearing and the legs to spin at about 70 rpm (or more), you should do so. Slower strokes increase heart rate, energy cost and perceived exertion—you'll have less oomph when you really need it.

Concentrate on pedaling circles (even though science types tell us that it's impossible), evenly applying pressure, then pulling all the way through each revolution. If your heels are raised at the bottom of the stroke, you're probably not doing this.

3. Use different muscles. On long climbs, move back and forth on the saddle. Slide to the rear to use more of your butt muscles (the glutes), which is less efficient but delivers more power. Slide forward and you use more of your leg muscles. Here's another way to think of it: With your upper body bent at about 45 degrees, you use mostly butt muscles. Sit more upright and you work the thighs. Switch regularly to rest each set.

4. Learn how to breathe. Concentrate on letting your stomach hang down, or deliberately push it out as you exhale. Also, exhale forcefully and inhale passively (the opposite of the typical pattern). These techniques improve airflow and keep you from panting. The pain and strain of climbing often cause riders to hold their breath or take uneven gasps.

Respiration can also be a powerful pacing tool. Synchronize your breaths with your pedal strokes (not necessarily one-to-one). On all but the shortest or steepest climbs, climbing is as much about rhythm as strength.

5. Plan ahead. On technical climbs you ride more slowly than normal, which means that finding the good line is more important. Any obstacle is a momentum thief, and you are already momentum-poor.

Pick your next three or four moves as you complete one. This will help you avoid surprises that would simply be inconvenient on the flats or downhill but will stop you on a climb. A slightly harder uphill line is better than an easy one that leads to immobility.

6. Ride shallow. You can take two arcs through an ascending curve. The inside line is shorter—but steeper and usually harder. As you go farther outside, the pitch gets shallower. Ride here. Many beginners think the slightly longer path is a disadvantage. It ain't.

Ride the
Bungee !

7. Ride straight. Well, as straight as you can. Weaving should be a last resort for conquering that steep dirt road. The slightest turn—a 1-degree steering angle—increases your rolling resistance about 6 percent. A 3-degree variation raises it 30 percent. Psychologically, riding straight is harder. Physically, it isn't. Shut up, brain.

8. Ride the bungee. More mind games—but this time, listen. Frank Lake, an expert-class NORBA (National Off-Road Bicycle Association) racer, taught me this at a Peak Performance climbing clinic. It helps long climbs go quicker, and it's a real psyche saver when you think you're cooked. Pick an object that's 10 to 30 yards up the trail. Throw a mental bungee cord around it and pull yourself up to the object with the cord. Then attach it to another distant anchor. It sounds silly to me even now, but it works.

9. Use bar-ends. You probably already know that these extensions are great for pumping the bike up a steep section. You stand, put your hands on the ends, and rock the bike with the leverage. But you can benefit from bar-ends even when you aren't cranking the bike from side to side. The wider position opens your chest and helps you breathe easier. Just make sure you aren't clenching.

10. Row, row, row your bike. Gently up the wall. When skills ninja John Olsen visited our Emmaus, Pennsylvania, office, in one ride he taught me what two years of home study hadn't: how to climb way-steep hills.

Stay seated, scooting forward until the tip of the saddle is—there's no way to put this delicately—wedged between your butt cheeks. You're not so much sitting on the saddle as you are merely contacting it. With each pedal stroke, pull back and down on the handlebar. The rowing motion combined with your position keeps both wheels dug.

Don't worry if you're not even close to succeeding. It's not something you can do just a little and then lose. It suddenly clicks and you can do it continuously. The most common mistake is not sticking the saddle where it must go. It's worth it. Really.

Finding Your Balance
between Gripping and Slipping

CLIMBING ON ⑮
LOOSE SURFACES

By Hank Barlow

Traction is always chancy when climbing in the dirt. All you can count on is a surface that might instantly slip from under your tires. Making the situation worse are super-low gears, because their tremendous torque promotes rear-wheel spin. Go ahead—downshift into a 24 × 32-tooth granny gear, stand up and pound the pedals. The rear wheel will break traction regardless of chainstay length or tire-tread pattern.

Unless, that is, you learn to balance on the edge of your power. An exquisitely fine line exists between holding and losing traction. Apply too much force and it's gone; use too little and you'll stall. It's akin to balancing on a gymnast's beam. If you stay centered you'll stay up. But lose that center and you fall.

That's how it is when climbing a steep grade with a loose surface. If you remain balanced on the bike and apply just enough power to keep moving, you won't break traction. But lose that delicate center by applying too much or too little power, or by leaning too far one way or another, and, like the gymnast, you'll fall.

Obviously, there are other factors at work here, too. Momentum, the product of mass and velocity, is one. It's a useful force in mountain biking and one of the favorite climbing ploys of experienced riders. But others badly misuse it. I often see riders flinging themselves into hills at maximum speed. Their legs spin wildly as they attempt to whirl up the hill, but they rarely succeed—not because momentum doesn't work, but because they are out of balance. When their momentum is exhausted, they are unable to pick up where it leaves off.

I learned this lesson on a beautiful slickrock line near Moab. The

If you select the right gear and resume pedaling at the perfect time, the transition into a steep climb can be nearly unnoticeable.

trick was the generous application of momentum. But I found out that if too much momentum is used, tires bounce wildly on the humps, bumps and ledges of the ascent. This left me out of control and wasting precious energy as my bike took its own zig-zag line up the hill. Finally the wheel turned at such a sharp angle that I was forced off the bike. Too little momentum, on the other hand, caused me to quickly click out of my pedal to keep from falling over as my bike crept to a standstill.

There are two keys to cleaning that climb. The first is carrying just enough momentum for a smooth passage up the initial pitch, but not so much that your bike reacts to the terrain changes. The second is being in a gear that matches the speed at which your pedaling resumes when momentum fades. If you're in too high a gear, you won't be able to keep cranking up the rest of the grade. If you're geared too low, you won't be able to start pedaling until almost all momentum is lost, and you're likely to spin the rear wheel in the effort to regain speed.

The transition from coasting to pedaling has to flow smoothly, and the power you apply has to be balanced between maintaining traction and accelerating. When timed just right, your first stroke blends so well with the bike's rapidly disappearing momentum that you never notice the end of one force and the beginning of the next. Your power is perfectly balanced.

PRACTICING POWER

To learn how to balance on the edge of your power, find a relatively steep hill with a moderately loose surface. This should be a climb you could handle quite easily if not for the lack of traction. Shift into your lowest gear and aggressively attack the hill. Get out of the saddle and force the rear wheel to begin breaking free. Do this a few times, then try it while sitting. Learn how much pedaling force you can apply before losing traction.

Now change tactics. Ride into the hill as slowly as you can in your lowest gear. Creep up so you're constantly on the verge of stalling. Pretend you're in an airplane, the stall warning buzzer keeps going off and you have to make the minimum adjustment to shut it up. Try this standing, then sitting.

Now pick the smallest cog you can ride up the slope in. Repeat the previous exercises. Pay attention to your stalling point. Work on sensing the loss of traction before it happens. Do it in and out of the saddle. Play with it. Have fun balancing on the point of power.

Now for the final ingredient: your arms. Shift into your granny gear and again ride into the hill slowly, trying to spin the rear wheel. But this time, counteract the force of your pedaling by pulling back and down on the handlebar. Pivot your hands and lower your wrists and elbows so your forearms are parallel to an imaginary line between your hubs. Get out of the saddle in a low crouch, your butt hovering over it. Feel how pulling back on the handlebar helps oppose your thrusts on the pedals.

Notice how you can control tire slip with your arms. Each time you push a pedal down, pull back on the handlebar and feel how the rear wheel is squashed into the dirt. As you reach the bottom of the stroke, relax your arms, thrust the bike forward, then resume pulling on the handlebar the moment you initiate the next stroke. Try this in different gears.

Now you're ready to increase the challenge. Find a steeper hill with an even looser surface. Shift into your lowest gear and slowly ride into the climb. Feel for the balance point that encompasses the power applied to each pedal stroke, the pull on the handlebar and the limit of the rear tire's traction. Don't worry about riding all the way up, but go as far as you can with the wheel on the verge of slipping. If it spins a tad, instantly adjust and regain traction without stopping. Feel how you can balance on the edge of your power. Try it in different gears, experiment and apply these techniques on each tough climb you ride.

DOWNHILL ⑯
THRILLS

By Hank Barlow

You're stoked. It's your first time on singletrack, and it isn't nearly as difficult as you imagined. All your fears (most of them, anyway) have been forgotten. You're riding smoothly, even effortlessly at times, and you just climbed a steep hill without dabbing. The trail bends past a small grove of aspens, flinches around the rotting remains of a fire-scarred fir . . . and disappears downward. Whoa! You hop off and stare at the descending tire tracks, realizing that other riders have made it. But can you?

Relax. Fear of tumbling over the handlebar has been felt by every rider. We've all wondered how the heck we were going to get down in one piece. You'll learn. Downhills are potentially dangerous, but also exhilarating. Arriving at the point where you look forward to them requires patience, caution and mastering a few basic skills. Most are merely adaptations of the same ones required for climbing and negotiating twisting singletrack. The keys are balance and braking.

BETTER BALANCE

In cycling, balance refers to your weight distribution between the front and rear wheels. On a flat surface when sitting in the saddle, more weight rests on the rear wheel than on the front. How much depends on your bike's frame geometry and your build and posture, but a typical ratio is 60:40 in favor of the rear.

A person's center of mass is located near the belly button. If a perpendicular arrow were hung there, it would point to a spot between the balls of your feet when you're standing on a flat floor.

Wanna cheat gravity? Slide back for balance.

When you're on a bike on a flat surface, it would point to a spot between the tires near the bottom bracket. As the surface is tilted upward (as when climbing), the arrow would swing backward toward the rear wheel's contact patch with the ground. Keep tilting, and eventually the arrow would pass through this point and you'd tip over backward.

The opposite happens as the surface is angled downward. The mythical arrow moves forward until it passes the front wheel, and you're unceremoniously spilled over the handlebar. It's easy to prevent this, though. Since the arrow is suspended from your center of mass, you can counteract its forward movement by sliding back on the saddle. On extremely steep descents, this may require moving back so far that your butt is off the saddle and suspended over the rear wheel. Another trick is to lower the saddle, but this is usually necessary only for extended downhills that are extremely steep or require navigating lots of rocks and logs. Usually, sliding back is enough. (Beware of going too far, though, because an unweighted front wheel will ignore your attempts to steer it.)

EFFECTIVE BRAKING

The next goal is controlling speed. Anticipate the descent by braking, just as you prepare for a climb by downshifting. It's better to start down too slow than too fast. Don't be afraid to use the front brake. Do respect its power, though. Compared with the rear, this brake will slow or stop you more effectively and suddenly because weight moves forward. (It's the same reason that car makers put disk brakes on front wheels and drums in back.)

Remember how your center of mass moves toward the front wheel as the bike tilts down? Applying the brakes has the same effect. The imaginary arrow pendulums forward like coffee in a cup when you decelerate in your car. This weight shift needs to be counteracted, and this is another reason to slide rearward on the saddle. You might hear this referred to as "staying behind the front brake."

Only use the rear brake lightly enough to prevent the wheel from locking. A skidding tire won't slow you effectively, but it will raise havoc with trails, creating grooves where water travels and erodes. When you sense the rear wheel skidding, immediately lighten your pressure on the brake lever.

Anticipate natural braking forces such as rocks, logs, sand and mud. You can use these to help slow the bike, but hitting them while the front brake is applied can send you flying. Once again, the remedy is anticipation. Lighten your pressure on the lever as the front wheel reaches the obstacle. Stay back on the saddle and allow momentum to carry you up and over and through. When the front wheel is clear, reapply its brake as necessary.

Although speed on a descent can be frightening, it can also be a wonderful ally. Speed translates into momentum, and momentum can get you through obstacles that you'd otherwise need to dismount for. Consequently, don't be surprised when you find yourself tiptoeing a delicate line between enough speed to get you through and too much for safety.

A classic example is on the Poison Spider Trail near Moab, Utah, one of the gnarliest, most challenging rides I've tried. Those who come closest to cleaning it are usually carrying more speed. Those who dab the most are the ones who try to finesse their way down and lack enough momentum to roll over rocks. But the consequences of failing are severe enough to deter all but the most aggressive riders. Lots of us prefer to err on the side of slow-motion dismounts.

Fat, soft tires also help on descents. They provide more cushioning and greater traction, and their weight helps keep the bike upright at slow speeds. But beware of sharp rocks if you ride with underinflated tires. When you're about to hit one, release some brake and simultaneously shift weight back to help the front tire ride up and over. Otherwise, you may drive it into the rock and execute a flying-forward dismount or get a pinch flat, which occurs when the top-down force of riding or jumping pinches the tire between the rim and an obstacle (like a rock). Help the back wheel follow by staying off the lever to generate some momentum. If you mess up, remember that you're better off failing to get the back wheel over than the front.

The final ingredient is practice. The more you ride down hills, the better your balance, technique and confidence will become. But if you get to a descent that you're not sure you can handle, walk down. Attempting to get off in the midst of a descent increases the risk of a tumble over the handlebar. There's no sense ruining a fine ride because your ego drives you down a slope that'll almost certainly cause a fall. You'll ride it someday. Meanwhile, relax, have fun and be patient as you develop your skills.

FRONT BRAKE PRIMER 17

By John Olsen

Sooner or later, every biker discovers the power of the front brake. In the worst case, this occurs when approaching a scary dip at the bottom of a hill. In a moment of panic, the rider gives a mighty squeeze on the lever and is flung into the scary dip face-first. Beginner's luck was invented to allow people to survive such violent learning experiences, but they are only allowed a few before paying a visit to Dr. Pain.

Too often the mishap causes riders to regard the front brake with fear and loathing. They go forth filled with the wisdom of experience, relying solely on the rear brake for all stopping duties. On even moderate hills they skid the back tire, digging a great gouge in the surface of the trail. This necessitates avoiding steep or slippery descents, because the locked rear wheel's braking power is minimal. Meanwhile, skilled mountain bikers who see them defacing the landscape under marginal control shake their heads and vow to keep well away from the malefactors.

The truth is, the best mountain bikers rely largely on their front brakes during any descent or when stopping hard. In fact, the steeper the hill or harder the stop, the more a skilled rider uses the front brake. The trick is to balance the two brakes gently and skillfully rather than using them as one might tug at the ejection lever in a burning jet fighter.

PHYSICS LESSON

When you coast down a 10-degree hill using your brakes to maintain 20 mph, you're dissipating about 2 horsepower, or five

times what your legs and lungs can sustain while climbing the same hill. Given this fact, you can see the potential for trail damage that could occur by skidding. There is a lot of force involved.

Even when you decelerate on level ground, your body weight pitches forward onto the front wheel. As you brake harder, more weight transfers forward until the back wheel rises off the ground.

The amount of braking force that a tire can transmit to the ground depends mainly on the amount of weight pressing it down. So as the rear wheel lightens during braking, it becomes easier to lock. In effect, the rear wheel's braking force is self-limiting: At some level of deceleration it will skid, and no more force will be available. The rear wheel will also

Don't do this! While too much front braking force can cause an endo, relying only on the rear brake to stop your descent leads to trail-damaging skids that will also erode your control.

be lightened by the effects of a downward slope, so that even less effort is needed to lock it. On the steepest descents just a light touch on the brake levers will do the trick.

FOCUS ON THE FRONT

The front brake is the answer to all these woes. As the pool of braking force available from the rear wheel dries up under deceleration, the front wheel's stopping potential rises. The rider's weight is smashing the front tire into the dirt, giving it almost limitless braking potential. In fact, it's restricted only by the rear-wheel liftoff (and the subsequent face plant).

The steepest controlled descent and the hardest stops can be made by modulating the front brake so that the rear wheel is just this side of liftoff. Meanwhile, the rider must decrease pressure on the rear brake lever to keep that wheel from locking.

How do you learn this fine art? Find a relatively harmless environment that's smooth, wide and moderately steep—such as a road up the side of a gravel pit. Wear enough protective gear to minimize damage in the event of a slow-motion tumble over the bar. Keep toe clips or clipless pedals loose.

Ride down the slope as slowly as possible, experimenting with both brakes. Go over the edge of the slope at a walking pace so that the front wheel doesn't flop to one side as you start down. Keep your weight back by sliding toward the rear of the saddle. Increase pressure on the rear brake until you sense that the tire is sliding, then back off slightly. Go down the slope several times this way, learning to get the most out of the rear brake and keeping the wheel just this side of lockup. You'll find that you need to constantly vary pressure on the lever as the slopes and surface change.

Now concentrate on the front brake (but use both). As you increase lever pressure, do two things: First, stiffen your arms to keep yourself from being thrown forward and to keep the front wheel from tearing the bar from your hands or turning. Second, lower your torso and slide your butt farther rearward—even off the back of the saddle. Ride down the hill at a walking pace and steer by shifting your torso from side to side, not by turning the bar, which could cause an unsightly endo.

Slow yourself repeatedly with the front brake, being sensitive to what the rear wheel is doing. If it locks up with even a little rear lever pressure, you're probably about to lift the rear wheel.

THE NOSE WHEELIE

When you feel good about your ability to control the bike's steering and speed while using the front brake, then you're ready to deliberately raise the rear wheel, a cool move called a nose wheelie. Lift your feet slightly to initiate it. Moving your torso forward helps, too. Play around with it.

A controlled nose wheelie is an elegant steering method useful for maneuvering through tight switchbacks. It looks cool, too.

Squeeze mostly the front
brake, straighten your arms
(to steady yourself and the
front wheel) and slide your
butt backward. To steer,
shift your torso sideways
instead of turning the bar.

Don't be too tentative. The point at which the bike will tip too far forward and dump you is much farther than most riders imagine.

In fact, it might be helpful for you to find this balance point on level ground—where a planned, slow-speed endo is least likely to do you harm. Again, experiment; it'll improve your chances of rolling (or running) away from an endo injury-free, make you less fidgety about the height of your nose wheelie and increase your control. For instance, you'll discover that simply releasing the front brake and letting the wheel roll will take you out of some scary-high nose wheelies.

Once you're comfortable doing a nose wheelie, try twisting your torso and pushing sideways with your feet to put the rear wheel down a few inches to one side or the other. This is an elegant, advanced steering method that's useful for tight switchbacks, because you can deliberately lift the rear wheel and place it on a new line.

Continue to improve your newfound skills by riding down your practice hill as slowly as possible, always modulating pressure on both levers as needed, and shifting your weight forward and back, left and right.

A skillful descent of a steep, slippery hill is a pleasure, and the skills you learn here will help you on the faster, wide-open stuff. Practice this as much as you can. For reasons of personal safety and trail etiquette, no mountain biking skill is as important.

TAKING TURNS ⑱

By Bill Strickland

I remember my first good turn. I thought I was wrecking. When the singletrack sliced sharp right, my mountain bike didn't. Inertia and my angle of approach had me riding a fat arc that would curve off the trail. Into trees and sticker bushes and rocks.

You gotta love desperation. Without knowing exactly why, I pointed my right elbow and knee out. There was this unsettling shifting sensation beneath me (the thing felt alive, I swear) as the bike abandoned our errant flight path and dived safely into the turn.

"That was better," said the guy who was sitting inside the corner and coaching me through each time. "That was good. You're getting the feel."

Great. So turning should feel like wiping out. It should feel like your bike is doing things you don't understand. Sounds like this technique needs a new PR campaign, no? After all, it is one of the most important basic skills.

Without it, I fell behind on group rides every time we threaded an un-straight section. Not much, but enough to make me work to catch up. Fatiguing and frustrating.

And there was the fear. I was afraid of turning on dirt. The way the wheels skitter and slip even when I'm riding straight and upright, I just couldn't get myself to lay into much of a lean. But fear can be useful. It slows you to a safe speed, for instance. But I think the best mountain bikers get their caution from respect—exploring their limitations instead of ignoring them.

"Okay," said the dirthead. "Now follow me. Watch what I do and try to copy it."

So I did, and then he followed me and shouted instructions, and

Off-camber Turn

WRONG!

then I followed him and then he followed me and shouted some more, and I got a little better. Then I followed him and wrecked because I thought I was better than I was.

The tumble didn't matter. I'd begun to understand this strange science, and that would have been worth a hundred spills to me. Who knows, it still might end up costing that many. But maybe I can save you from one or two. Follow me through this twister.

YOUR TURN

The principles we'll use to negotiate this wide, level curve form a solid foundation of cornering knowledge. The ideas change slightly with the terrain—and from what I understand, some of the moves become outmoded once you get really good. But for now, these seven steps improve safety and control while letting you zip through at higher speeds.

1. If possible, plan your path to approach wide, cut inside across the turn and exit wide. This old roadie technique reduces the sharpness of the curve and minimizes the amount of lean you'll need. It also lets you ride a more direct line (you go almost straight through the curve instead of turning), which helps traction on loose surfaces. Of course, you won't often have this luxury off-road. Your line is usually determined by the width or condition of the trail.

Off-camber Turn

Right!

2. Brake before the turn. Whenever I approach with great intentions and speed (great for me, anyway), I geek out because I'm going too fast. Locking the levers in a turn makes us more likely to skid. Even if we don't cuddle the dirt blanket, our rhythm and swoop are disrupted. It's more efficient and, for some reason, quicker to brake before entering a curve. For instance, a rider who surfs an entire turn at a smooth 15 almost always gets through quicker than one who enters at 17 and brakes.

3. Stop pedaling and keep your cranks horizontal. Unless you think you'd enjoy catching a pedal on a bank, rock or log. On smooth surfaces, however, you can keep the outside pedal down to improve traction (see step 5).

4. Lean into the turn. Press down on the grip that's on the inside and angle the bike over. At slow speeds, or for tighter corners, you'll need to steer slightly inward, too. Don't worry about being tentative and not getting much lean. As you gain confidence in your traction, you'll slant more. The key is to slowly build speed and lean. Too much of a jump in either, and you'll skid.

5. As you lean, stick your bike to the ground with body weight. This creates additional traction. Used correctly, your weight can drive the treads into the surface and counteract the sideways forces that want to push your bike out from under you. One method is to push down against the outside pedal. Some riders stay seated and transfer their weight straight down through the seatpost. Others move the bike underneath them until it's on the inside track and their body rests outside. Even the opposite—bike outside, body inside—can be effective.

What's the best method? It depends on your speed, your tires, your mojo, the turn, the terrain . . . The point is that few beginners use any method. Play with them all until you find one that seems to work naturally.

6. If needed, correct your line with elbow and knee

swings. Especially at first, you will ride too wide—the problem I described earlier. When this happens, your instinct is to crank the handlebar inward. Sometimes this works, but sometimes it turns the front tire in a direction your momentum doesn't want to go. Things get messy. Instead, pop your limbs out toward the inside corner. It's swoop time.

7. Accelerate out. Jam on your pedals sometime after passing the apex but while you're still in the arc. Do it right, and you'll feel as if the turn is flinging you out onto the trail. You can learn to recognize the right moment by practicing on a smooth (and preferably soft) turn. Try to begin pedaling closer and closer to the turn's midpoint. Don't feel flung? You're waiting too long. If you stick a pedal in the ground, or find speed but lose it before exiting, you're not waiting long enough.

THE LEARNING CURVE

Not a bad turn. But why did you skid? In order of frequency, here are the mistakes that beginners make.

Too little lean or weighting to maintain traction. We just can't believe a bicycle will hold that well on uncertain surfaces. But it will—in some instances, the traction is better than that of an upright bike. Just trust physics, and your bike. Lean and press. Lean and press.

Too little confidence. The bike makes adjustments on its own. To the uninitiated, these feel like wipeouts-in-waiting. So we bail. Ride it out. You'll be surprised.

Too tough of a turn. These tips are ideal for wide, level corners or banked curves—beginner fare. We need other moves for sharp turns, off-camber corners (which fall downhill on the outside) and much-littered, washboarded or rutted turns. Hone your basic skills on the easy stuff.

Too much speed. If you feel like you're doing everything right but you still can't stick the turns like the rest of the group, then don't. You're a novice. Enjoy it while you can. Someday you'll be expected to ice every move.

SPEED RACERS ⓭

By Bill Strickland

So I was standing there at the West Virginia Fat Tire Festival in Slatyfork, watching these racers climb a hill I'd have trouble getting over in a helicopter. And this guy rolled up, stopped to spectate, and we started talking. Aren't these trails great? Why aren't you racing?

After a while, the guy noticed that the bug-eyed character painted on the head tube of my Klein is the same manic little dude that skids through the pages of Mountain Bike magazine each month. He asked if I supply the words. I admitted that I do.

He says, "You know your problem?"

I know lots of my problems. But I didn't know which one he meant, so I said, "No, what?"

"Everything you write about is slow. Slow moves, slow hops, slow, slow, slow. Dude, some of us go fast. For once write about that."

SOMETIMES FASTER IS SAFER

I don't do much about fast skills because I don't go fast. But I should. For one thing, fast is fun—even when it's terrifying. For another, fast raises the stakes. It tests your limits, which is the best way to improve. Finally, even if you don't like to ride fast, you should have the ability to because sometimes it's necessary. Certain trail conditions are actually safer or easier to conquer when you're speeding.

So here are some quick thoughts on going quicker.

Momentum helps. Momentum is your pal. You just might not know

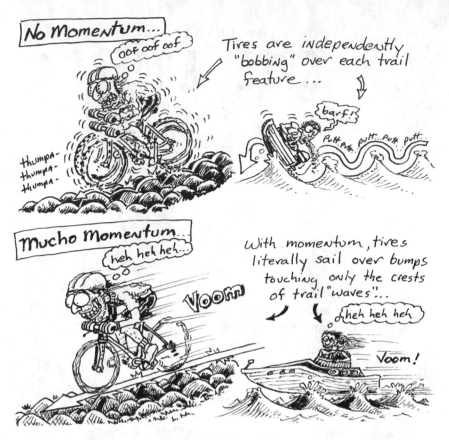

it yet. There's this local climb covered with loose rocks about the size of—I hate saying this, but that's what everyone calls them—baby heads. I used to ride slower than normal on the baby heads. It made me feel like I wasn't hurting them as bad, and I thought I'd have more control. But I always dumped. Then one time we were doing that mock-racing kind of thing. I slammed into the baby heads way too fast. And, of course, I rode up without ever putting a foot down. Clean.

Inertia is as much a cycling tool as balance or fitness. It'll get you through a lot of things. If there's a section that you're having trouble with, maybe you're going too slow. Grit your teeth and try going just one or two miles per hour faster. Momentum does other cool stuff, too, like turning marginal bunny-hops (mine, for instance) into cloud-banging flights.

The Magic Speed Barrier. An expert-class off-road racer I know has a theory about why great racers look like they're floating over stuff that destroys the rest of us. They've broken the Magic Speed Barrier.

We all have a pace we maintain most of the time—an average speed. (It's possible to go faster, but this is where we mostly ride.)

Any tiny gain in average speed takes tons of practice and dedication. So it could take me years to go from being a 10mph rider to a 12.5mph rider.

But at some point you hit the Magic Speed Barrier (which is slightly different for everyone). If you get past this, amazing speed increases are possible. For instance, once I raise my average to 13 mph, I'll be able to do 15 mph immediately, for about the same amount of effort and skill. The Barrier is where loads of finesse and finagling are replaced by sheer speed and momentum. You don't need to miss stuff because you ride right over it.

The point is, don't get discouraged if you try to become faster but don't see much progress. You're working your way toward magic.

Small movements. Big speed must be controlled by big reactions, right? Nope. Go out and watch birds. When they fly slowly they make big, sweeping movements with their wings to change direction. But when they swoop or dive, they accomplish the same amount of directional change just by twitching a single feather.

Be a bird. As your speed increases, your bike and body adjustments should become smaller. It's easy to get pumped and overreact in even a simple turn, or yank the bike way the heck up in the air when that's not at all a good thing. When speeding, be spare and graceful. Demolition-derby drivers flail. Formula One racers caress.

How to accelerate. We all need to develop a kick, whether it's to win a race at the line or zip over a short but steep hill. One way is simply to honk on the pedals and get your power up. This works, but it can blow your legs. Spinning faster is more efficient than putting more force into your pedal strokes.

Try this next time you want to surge: Shift to an easier gear and increase your pedal cadence. Just before you spin out (pedal as fast as you can), shift to a harder gear. Repeat this until you're at top speed.

You probably won't need to shift to the easier gear once you get the feel. And if you're super-strong, you can forget this and just jam. This is an easy and clear way for novices to learn the relation between spinning and speeding.

How fast should you go? I can't answer this one with a number. My guess is that most beginners go a little slower than they should. A few who were born rad go too fast for their skill level—when they need to bail they won't be able to. Some of us are just about right.

It's dumb to get hung up on numbers anyway. No matter what your speed capability is now, improving it is a worthy goal.

The first step is to figure out what's holding you back. For some of us—especially brand-new mountain bikers—the missing ingredient is nerve. Others lack the fitness to sustain speed. And some of us simply don't have the skills we need.

Identifying your weakness will help you get rid of it. At first, I used to turtle along whether I was on a wide-open dirt road or a twisty singletrack. I was scared.

But I concentrated on getting acclimated and it worked. I realized that certain situations are safer than others. I could go faster on smooth terrain with little risk—but I kept the same slow pace on tough stuff. My speed was being suppressed by trail conditions.

Now I'm learning to increase my speed even on the nasty trails. Through repetition, I'm beginning to go faster over things that used to stop me. And as my technique improves, I also feel my fitness level increasing.

You might not follow the exact same progression, but there will be definite steps. Just stick with it. Pay attention to why you go slowly.

Okay—here's the humiliating part. How fast do I really go? I've been mountain biking more than a year and most of my riding barely breaks double digits. I've been over 40 mph on a mountain bike once. On a long, smooth downhill that I've done about 800 times, I go about 18 mph.

SHOCKING ADVICE ⓴

By Hank Barlow

Do bikes equipped with suspension systems—front, rear or both—require different riding techniques than unsuspended bikes? No and yes. No, because the way a bicycle moves is a direct response to a rider's position over it. Lean left and the bike, suspended or not, turns left. Lean right and it turns right. Yes, because the way you distribute your weight on a suspended bike is different than on an unsuspended one.

The extent of these weight shifts depends on the degree of suspension. Bikes with minimal suspension, such as a Moots with its shock-absorbing mono-seatstay, hardly feel different than standard bikes and don't require much. At the other extreme are bikes with suspensions supple enough to roll over railroad tracks without a road crossing.

So, yes, you'll have to learn how to ride a suspension bike, or to be more precise, you'll have to modify your technique to match your suspension's functions. But the basic rider positioning and movements remain the same, suspended or not.

UP FRONT

The primary difference in riding a bike with a front suspension is the reduced need to unweight the front end. On an unsuspended bike, you either loft the front wheel over obstacles or maneuver around them; but with a front suspension you can simply continue pressing down on the handlebar, let the suspension do the work and roll over obstacles. In fact, it's a good idea not to loft the front end until you're thoroughly familiar with the suspension's handling.

Your rig's suspension can't absorb all the shock from a sharp transition. Flexing your arms and legs can help.

There are three good reasons for this. First, in lofting the front end, the first move is typically pressing down hard on the bar to compress the front tire and produce an upward springing action.

But in pressing down on a suspension fork, you won't create that rebound effect; you'll just use some, or even all, of the fork's travel. If your timing is off, you could slam into the obstacle with, in effect, no front suspension.

Second, for the suspension to work, it has to have something to work against. That's you. If you loft the front end, you've eliminated that opposing force, and the front wheel will simply bounce off the obstacle as if there were no suspension.

Finally, steady downward pressure on the handlebar (different from the abrupt compression described earlier) helps settle the front wheel after it's passed over the obstacle.

But a suspension-equipped fork doesn't eliminate the need for the rider's active participation. Each suspension system has a specific amount of travel, generally in the range of three to four inches. Once that full range of travel is used, there's no more suspension. Therefore, if you slam into an obstacle that's ten inches high with a fork that has four inches of travel, you're going to run out of travel, and the front end will have to bounce up to get over the obstacle. So the rider will have to create the clearance by absorbing the bounce with his arms, then shifting weight forward. True, the impact will be muted by the fork's initial action, but the residual shock will still have to be absorbed.

You absorb this shock by riding with flexed arms and a firm grip on the handlebar. (Sounds a lot like riding an unsuspended bike, doesn't it?) Depending on the size of the obstacle, shift some weight back—but not much—and let the wheel bang into it. When the wheel rises, let it come up to you by flexing your arms as if you're dropping your torso down toward the bike. The moment the wheel is over the obstacle, press firmly down on the handlebar and shift weight forward again to ease the rear wheel's passage (assuming your bike has no rear suspension).

Naturally, all this happens with lightning speed, hopefully in one fluid movement, not in segments, as my description may seem to indicate. Just remember that your objective is to minimize your torso's up and down movements relative to terrain changes.

WATCH YOUR REAR

Probably the most common problem that riders with front suspensions encounter is slamming their rear wheels. They forget that it has to pass over the same obstacles as the front but without the benefit of a suspension. If the rider remains firmly planted in the saddle, the rear wheel may smash into an obstacle, and the result can be a pinch flat or even a crumpled wheel. To avoid such damage, the rear wheel has to be lightened. Accomplish this by riding with flexed legs and lifting your butt off the saddle just before impact. Higher tire air pressure helps, too.

If your bike has a rear suspension, the problem of back damage isn't a worry. Remain seated and allow the rear spring to do its thing. Just as with the front, the rear suspension needs something to work against and that's you, or rather your weight, pressing down. But again, the size of the obstacle affects your preparation. If the obstacle is large, you'll have to get out of the saddle to allow the rear wheel to bounce up and over without damage or loss of control.

CLIMBING POINTS

When climbing, the only technique difference that a suspended bike demands is the ability—some say the requirement—to remain seated. But you still need to shift forward on the saddle to keep enough weight on the front wheel for steering. On extreme climbs, scoot forward onto the tip of the saddle, pivot your wrists down, drop your elbows, stay seated and hammer, but always smoothly. Don't worry about picking a line around obstacles since the suspension enables you to roll over them.

Out-of-the-saddle climbing on a suspension bike demands as smooth a pedaling action as possible to minimize bouncing. Keep your body centered and stable. Don't rock because this may cause the suspension to bounce and interfere with its movement over the ground.

Cornering can be affected by suspension, but generally only at high speeds. The force of diving fast into a hard turn can compress the suspension and alter the way the bike handles because the head angle and trail have changed. Fortunately, I've found this to be a hypothetical problem that rarely occurs on the trail.

All in all, riding a suspension-equipped bike doesn't require any drastic changes in riding technique, just subtle modifications. It takes time to learn the characteristics of whatever suspension you select. Don't take a new suspension immediately to the max with the assumption that it will suddenly and magically turn you into a high-speed gonzo expert. Begin as if you're still riding without a suspension and slowly get a feel for how yours reacts. Remember, suspensions allow higher speeds that can translate into jarring crashes when you suddenly discover you're way over your head in the speed zone. Concentrate on riding smoothly, and the speed will come.

Discover the Hidden Power
in Your Levers—Or Else

BRAKE OR BREAK ㉑

By Bill Strickland

Ouch. Did you hear that? The doctor told me my shoulder would probably make that creaking noise for the rest of my life.

I guess this means I'm a real mountain biker.

Before I crashed, I remember thinking "Man, I'm way, way out on my control curve." But at one point I had an epiphany about braking. I realized that I was *overbraking*—locking my levers too often and too easily, depriving myself of momentum and balance (and fun).

So when the dirt road kept going down, and the five guys with me kept going faster . . . well, I'd never felt like that on a mountain bike before. My emancipation from overbraking set me free. It was like what a very fast fish must feel like as it cuts through water—completely part of its element. If you've ever experienced that feeling, you know what I mean.

There are probably lots of reasons I couldn't get my front tire out of that in-curving rut in an out-curving corner. Overconfidence. Carelessness. Stupidity. Bad luck. But mostly I blame my braking style.

One of my buddies told me he maxed that hill at 32 mph. I had no business in that neighborhood. Not on that tricky descent. And not without better braking skills.

STOP RIGHT THERE

Here are five valuable pointers that I've gathered from experts.

1. Find a favorite hand position. This is a subject of some debate among dirtheads in the know. Some riders keep their thumbs and

3 Rear · O Front

Boggy Conditions

forefingers around the handlebar and use the other three fingers to brake. I've seen guys who put their index, middle and ring fingers on the lever, gripping the handlebar with their thumb and pinkie. There are other configurations, too, but I prefer the second position for the rear brake and a variation (index and middle on the lever; thumb, pinkie and ring finger gripping the bar) for the front. It feels secure and doesn't tire my fingers.

However you end up, make sure to settle on a position that's comfortable because your hands should almost always be there. Mountain biking is braking. You have to be ready anytime.

2. Learn to adapt your position. The number of fingers on the lever should change depending on the terrain. It has to do with how much handlebar control you need balanced with how much force your braking might require. Here are some common suggestions.

Mushy stuff (sand, gravel and mud). No fingers on the front, three on the rear. A braked front wheel is more likely to dig in and bog.

Way steep. Three front, three rear. This allows you to really torque on the front brake, which is a good idea when you're descending. It keeps you from skidding the rear wheel. Plus, the front brake packs more stopping power.

Anything else. Two front, three rear. This should keep you from overbraking in front, which usually results

Aiiieee

3 Front · 3 Rear

Way Steep

in a face plant. In a normal situation, you should apply both brakes at the same time, putting slightly more pressure on the back than the front at first, and increase the front squeeze as necessary. A handy rule to remember: "Brake hard where the ground is hard and soft where the ground is soft."

3. Brake with your entire bike. Your levers and cantilevers are only the most obvious parts of your stopping system. To increase control and power, it can help to grip the seat with your quads or move your weight back as you brake. You can also slow the bike by running up banks or curving turns. I'm told there are many subtle maneuvers like this that we'll discover only by shifting around ourselves and our bikes as we brake. Just as good mountain bikers use their entire bikes and bodies to steer, they go beyond fingers when it comes to stopping, too. Watch them and experiment.

4. Don't use your brakes only when you want to slow. Good braking is about control, and sometimes it can even help you build speed. Try alternating squeezes and releases on your next long descent. Lay off the brakes sooner than usual coming out of a corner. Notice the control it gives you? The surges of speed?

This is the hidden power of brakes. They do more than stop you. They help you master your movement. Eventually you can use this for all kinds of more advanced purposes, such as adjusting your balance on the fly and springboarding into gonzo moves.

5. If you use your bike as a support while you step along rocks to cross a stream, keep those levers locked. This is one that did happen to me. Just one more time mountain biking made me feel like a fish.

Six Tips for Never Tipping

BALANCING ACT ㉒

By Bill Strickland

Sometimes the simplest things make the biggest difference. Learning to balance motionless on a mountain bike was one of those things for me.

I'm not sure why I decided it was time to acquire that skill, but I know it had nothing to do with all the benefits I discovered. I'd always admired riders who stayed on their bikes at every stop, casually balancing in place while the rest of us plunked our feet down. I liked the friendly superiority inherent in the move. It seemed to me to be like juggling: If you can do it, you can't help showing off a little, but because it's such a cool activity, no one begrudges you the skill. In fact, everyone watching wishes they knew how.

In the same way, I think all of us aspire to be balancers. It's just one of those things.

Or so I thought.

I practiced my balancing act on and off for about four months before I got it down pat. There have been lots of embarrassments: slow-mo topples, sideways crash-and-burns, skinned knees, scraped hands, ripped grips, handlebar-size lawn divots . . .

There have also been a few stunning (at least to me) feats of equilibrium. One time I ran smooth and fluid as water through a series of dabless transitions between motion and unmotion. That will stick with me forever—as will the first time I broke the 30-second standstill barrier.

But the biggest surprise is how much this skill has helped me on the trail. I'm not only a better balancer, I'm a better mountain biker, all around, just because I learned what seemed to be only a neat trick.

WHEN BALANCE COMES IN HANDY

You know those times when you completely flub it and ram something you should have gone around or over? You won't automatically dab if you improve your balance. After your wheel rebounds and pitches you backward, you can catch your balance and hover for a few seconds, then find your pedal stroke and take another shot.

When a rock or a rut stops you, your shoes won't scramble for solid ground. You can hang with the situation for a little while—usually long enough to at least execute a controlled dab, and sometimes long enough to juke and pedal your way out of the whole mess. Another advantage is that you can pause to study the trail without disrupting the rhythm of the ride. Your wheelies will improve. You'll corner a little better. Catching air, landing, drifting across loose dirt, slipping on slick stuff—none of this will be as scary.

Learning to balance gives you more awareness of how the bike reacts to shifting weight. After you gain some of this knowledge at a standstill, your body and mind (or whatever you ride with) instinctively apply it while you're rolling, too.

THE SINGLETRACK STAND

The best way to improve your on-bike balance is through the technique that roadies call a trackstand (and that we might logically call a singletrack stand). It's that rarest of things: a combination of style and substance. Following are six steps for mastering this important skill.

1. Relax and ride loose. Grip the handlebar lightly, with your elbows and knees bent as you coast to a stop or lightly apply the front brake, whichever feels more comfortable.

2. Get on the good foot. The pedals should be horizontal (in the three- and nine-o'clock position) with your "good foot" forward. This is the foot you favor. It's usually on the same side as the hand you favor, but not always. If you're unsure, think about which foot you automatically put forward when you're coasting with the crankarms leveled. That's your good foot. Apply slight pressure to the pedal with this foot—just enough to inch the bike forward. At the same time, squeeze the front brake hard enough to prevent forward motion.

3. Turn toward the good foot. At the same time, turn the front wheel in the direction of your good foot. You'll probably oversteer at first. You just need enough angle to bring the bike into a stable position. You'll feel it when you're in the right spot.

4. Maintain equilibrium. You want to keep yourself in a kind of suspended state between rolling and falling. It's like an isometric exercise where muscle groups push against each other, working hard but not moving.

If you begin to fall in the direction of your good foot, turn the wheel straighter and ease off the brake and pedal. This rolls your weight (and sometimes the bike) back slightly and returns your balance.

If you begin to fall in the other direction, put more pressure on the pedal and lock up the brake. This shifts your force forward.

5. Use your knees. After you find a steady point, use your knees to maintain balance. If you begin to tip to one side, point the opposite knee out.

AT A STANDSTILL

Don't worry. None of this is as difficult to understand once you're on the bike. You'll comprehend what you should do in a few seconds. Of course, doing it is another matter. Don't expect much hang time in your first 20 to 30 attempts.

Thankfully, the learning curve may be long but it isn't steep. It's not like we're practicing ten-foot drop-offs at 30 mph. My worst injury was a scraped knee and bruised hand, and that was because I was stupid enough to practice on a sidewalk.

Use grass. It's soft, which means you can safely practice another skill: falling over without putting your hand out. Just stay with the bike as it tips, letting the handlebar and pedal take the impact. This habit could save you from a broken wrist someday.

It also helps to practice on a slight incline. Point yourself up, and gravity will help you find that state of equilibrium. Once you know what that feels like, move to level ground.

Maybe the greatest thing about learning to balance is that you can do it anywhere, for any amount of time. I've practiced for half an hour in my living room and for five seconds at a stoplight. You even find yourself practicing it without planning to, automatically balancing at a water stop or a fork in the trail. And one day, just as instinctively, you won't be practicing anymore. You'll be doing it.

CLICKING IN ㉓

By Bill Strickland

Have you heard this joke: "Clipless pedals aren't any harder to use than toe clips. In fact, they're easier." Experienced riders like to tell that one to us novices, and boy is it funny. It's so hilarious that my entire body hurts from laughing. Or maybe that omnipresent ache is from the gazillion pratfalls I've taken since I decided to go clipless.

During my two-month break-in period I landed on every exposed and helmeted inch of my skull. I skinned or sprained my elbows, shoulders, wrists, hip, knees, neck, nose, ear, butt, big toe (even I don't know how, but it hurts), little finger and assorted other parts. But it finally began to happen. I clicked in to clicking in. Just like the real riders.

Is it worth it? And should you do it?

Probably.

I know I should sound more enthusiastic. There's no question that climbing, speed, power and control improve with clipless pedals. It's not that you suddenly get more of these qualities. It's just that, like a fiber-optic phone line, clipless pedals are a more efficient transfer. You're able to draw an extra bit of ability out of yourself and put it into the bike. This newfound effort might be enough to let you loft your bike, stay with the speedy pack on group rides or conquer that long, steep killer hill.

But there's always a but. If you're happily casual, the hassle of clipless pedals will outweigh the benefit. They're more expensive and more complicated. The cleats (and pedal parts that engage them) wear with use and must be replaced. Your choice of riding shoes is limited—every time I have to search for my special Onza-cleated hooves before spinning to the grocery store or the pizza place, I think about how much I miss just grabbing my bike and pedaling away on whatever shoes I happened to be wearing.

Even if you're more hard-core, geography might make you content with toe clips. It's no secret that many excellent riders in wet or ultra-technical regions prefer traditional cages, a tendency that elicits scorn from equally excellent clipless honchos who claim that anything can be ridden locked in. This dissension confused me—which great-riding guru to believe?—until I realized it is mainly an East Coast/West Coast difference in philosophy disguised as a question of practicality. There is no answer. Ride what you want to ride and you'll ride well.

That's why I finally made the switch, and the only reason you should, too. I wanted to. Don't do it because someone thinks you should or because a hot rider tells you it's right for your region, or even because it's the hip gear. Going clipless is like deciding to find a new job. If you find yourself thinking about it more than you should, you know it's time.

RIDING THE CLIPLESS CURVE

I know clipless pedals will occasionally cost me some skin in eastern Pennsylvania's rockiest, loggiest technical sections. And I know they'll malfunction during our spring and winter mud seasons. But despite these specific drawbacks, I had hoped they would help me ride better overall. After a steep learning curve, they did.

There's no way around that curve. When you buy your setup you'll get plenty of advice for breaking your specific pedal in and for practicing the best engagement and disengagement techniques. Repetition and wrecks are the only way to master that important advice. But going clipless doesn't mean you need to go tipless. Here are six nuggets of advice that might ease the transition.

1. Try lots of pedals before you buy. Apart from saddles and mojos, there may be no more personal bike part. For instance, my trailmates terrorized me with horror stories about the Onza H.O.'s unpredictable release and engagement. But the pedal's stubborn streak never materialized, and it became my favorite. It's light, sheds mud, is simple to service and looks cool. Do not underestimate this last factor. Another company's stuff worked just as well in my limited test run, but because it looked boxy, I rode boxy. Or at least that's how I rationalized my choice.

2. Shave your sole. Instruction manuals explain how to mount your cleats, but I don't think that's enough. Click into your pedal, then take your foot out of the shoe. Flip it over and examine the whole thing. Treads that touch the pedal will interfere with your entry and release. Note the problem areas, then trim 'em with a razor knife or box cutter after unclicking the shoe. The offending treads would eventually wear away, but why wait?

3. Ride with stiffer shoes. Flexible soles also complicate entries and exits. I had to trade some of my favorite flexible hike-a-bike high-top Avias for stiff-soled versions from Nike, Specialized and Adidas. Sorry, old friends.

4. Don't forget to practice clicking in, too. Long after twisting out becomes second nature (panic can be a useful learning tool), you'll be flailing away during restarts. I still can't click in consistently. I suspect this is because the movement isn't instinctual. We have to think about it.

Most of my trouble comes from not putting my foot on the right part of the pedal—the cleat misses its mate. Last week I made a small mark on top of my shoe that aligns with the pedal spindle. When the mark is over the spindle, my cleats engage. This helps me avoid the step-and-guess game.

5. Commit fully or bail one second earlier. With clips and straps I could ride right to the rim of disaster and still have time to save myself with a dab. With clipless pedals, an additional second ticks off between my decision to dab and actual touchdown. A second doesn't seem like much until you're teetering on top of a wet log perched on a sidehill or slamming down a field of baby head–sized rocks. That delay caused some of my worst crashes. Experienced riders tell me it will eventually disappear (and they must be right—my original delay was like three seconds). But until it does, I've decided to either quit early (when I'm still safe but think I might wreck) or give it everything I've got. Mountain biking hurts more than it used to. But I also clean all kinds of things I thought I had no business even trying.

6. Carry extra cleat screws (and even an extra cleat, if possible). Jury-rigging a broken toe clip is easy. Riding with a loose cleat isn't. A great Colorado singletrack ride was nearly ruined when one of my screws buried itself in the dust. I didn't have extras but—tip 6a—I used a water bottle–cage bolt to tighten the cleat enough to click halfway in. Ain't this sport great?

Finally, don't worry. Clipless pedals aren't any harder to use than toe clips. In fact, they're easier.

And if you believe that, I have some singletrack on Mount Tam I'd like to sell you.

SEVEN SOLUTIONS TO SIMPLE SCREWUPS

By Hank Barlow

"Keep your eye on the ball." This favorite American sports mantra works just as well for mountain biking as it does for baseball or tennis. In fact, it's the antidote to one of our sport's most common errors.

But before you can apply such simple solutions to your mountain biking, you need to recognize your simple mistakes. Every rider makes them, but only the good ones learn to correct them. With this in mind, check out these seven common blunders—and the seven ways you can avoid them.

1. Looking at the wrong thing. Novices on singletrack usually run into the very objects they hope to avoid. The reason is that in their intensity to keep from hitting a rock or log, they stare at it. This is where your Little League coach was right. Keep your eye on the ball (or rock), and you'll hit it. The only difference is that in mountain biking, it's you, not the rock, that gets slammed.

Solution: Look at the path you want to take. Your front wheel will follow. Simple as that.

2. Staying in the saddle too much. The way that novice bikers keep their butts planted makes me wonder if seats are coming equipped with Super Glue. New riders seem to think their security is directly dependent upon their rears remaining on the saddle no matter what. Wrong.

The saddle transmits every jolt and vibration straight to your butt and spine. On rough ground, your eyes start feeling like Daffy Duck's after he's been smacked on the head.

Solution: Use your mountain bike's primary suspension system. I'm not talking about forks or seatposts, and I sure don't mean your

You might like the dip, but your chain and bearings won't. So carry your rig across water, if possible.

butt. I'm talking arms and legs. Your wrists, elbows, shoulders, ankles, knees and hips create a superbly flexible and efficient suspension system that does wonders to float your torso and head above the action.

But the equipment only works if you use it right. Leave your rear on the saddle, and you eliminate the suspension. Instead, stand up. Keep your legs and arms bent and loose and let them carry your weight. You can't ride this way all the time, of course, but do it when the terrain has you bouncing around.

3. Ignoring the front brake. Your real stopping power resides in your front brake. In fact, a skidding rear tire doesn't even slow you much, if at all. While it looks spectacular with all its accompanying dust, it only tears up the trail and wears out the tire. The steeper the descent, the more you need your front brake. The rear one should be employed lightly, just to keep the back wheel from locking.

Solution: As an exercise, practice using just the front brake on descents. This can be risky, so start slow. Feather the front brake, using it with respect. Clench too hard or stay too far forward, and you might exit over the handlebar. As you gain confidence, gradually increase your dependence on the front brake. Then practice, practice and practice some more.

4. Not drinking enough water. I can't begin to count all the people I've seen leaving for long mountain bike rides carrying only one small water bottle. It's hard to even find a mountain bike with brazeons for less than two bottles. Yet even in the desert around Moab, Utah, a place where dehydration lurks around every stone, I see people riding with just one.

You can die from not drinking enough, and even if you don't, a low fluid level can adversely affect your ability to ride, especially at high elevations.

Solution: Take the largest bottles you can buy and gulp either water or an energy drink several times an hour. It's better to drink all your liquid in the early stages than try to ration it for the ride's duration. And never wait until you're thirsty to drink. By then, your body is already way down the path to dehydration.

One effective method to make sure you're drinking enough is to monitor the color of your urine during a ride. If it's murky or yellow (or if you don't have to urinate at all), your intake is too low. If it's pale, you're doing fine. But don't wait until a pit stop to start hydrating. Drink early and often.

5. Riding without a tool kit. A roadie might survive with only a patch kit and a pump, but you will definitely need more—a pair of pliers, a screwdriver, Allen wrenches, a crescent wrench, a chain-rivet tool—stuff like that. The rivet tool is especially important because it can mean the difference between walking back and riding back.

Solution: Get the stuff I've mentioned above and learn to use it. Even before you learn, take it on rides. You might meet someone who knows what to do with it. If not, you'll probably be able to figure out some sort of repair that will get you home. Without a tool kit, this option doesn't exist.

6. Riding through water and sand. I know, charging into a stream is great fun, especially on a hot day. Water flies everywhere and you get soaked. But so does your bike and its bearings. This isn't so bad if you grease the bearings as soon as you get home. But be honest. Aren't you more likely to lubricate yourself with a beer when you get back? Meanwhile, the water goes to work and before long, bearings and races are corroded. Your chain also becomes weaker from the corrosion and will eventually decide to destruct in the midst of a particularly gnarly climb.

Sand is as bad as water and maybe even worse. Imagine all those fine steel balls smoothly rolling around in their coating of grease. Now add a little sand. Sort of like dragging your fingernails across a blackboard, isn't it? Save yourself substantial grief and take my word on the horrors of this.

Solution: Carry your bike or ride slowly across streams, puddles and sand. Otherwise, lubricate your bearings after every exposure and oil your chain before, during and after every ride.

7. Too much air pressure. Too many riders pump their tires until they're hard. Subsequently, they bounce more on every bump, increasing the roughness of the ride while decreasing control.

Solution: For traction and comfort you need fat, soft tires. The fatter they are, the lower the air pressure required. Other factors that affect your perfect pressure include weight, terrain and speed. Don't worry about pounds per square inch; use your thumb to check the rubber's squish factor. Experiment until you discover what works best. You'll know your tires are too soft if you start experiencing pinch flats. Add a bit more air and they'll be just right.

Skills

INSANE DROP-OFFS ㉕

By Captain Dondo

You're riding the contour of a hill when suddenly the trail turns straight down for a few yards, then continues to traverse. It looks ridiculously steep but the riders in front of you make it, so you know it's possible. Now it's your turn, but you balk and walk, or panic mid-drop and head over the handlebar. No, it's not the tires.

Next time do this.

 step 1 Approach the lip slowly enough to look over the brink, but not so slowly that you have to twitch the front wheel for balance. Take a quick mental trip down, avoiding any major front-wheel stoppers (rocks, roots) by not looking at them. Breathe in. Breathe out. Take a stroke to get going, then hold the pedals level and start lifting your butt off the saddle.

step 2

Slide your butt back as the front wheel drops in. Let the bike go first, then follow it. The front brake does nearly all the work, so don't use much rear. If either wheel skids, you'll slide off the good line.

step 3

Did you ever tip backward out of a chair? It happens because your center of gravity goes beyond the pivot point of the rear chair legs. Ditto with drop-offs (except you fall forward). Keep your hips behind the contact/pivot point of the front wheel by straightening your arms and legs and burying the saddle in your belly. Front brake finesse keeps the rear wheel rolling and on the ground.

Begin lifting your butt as you eyeball the transition back to flat-
ness. If the exit is abrupt, you'll have to let go of the front
brake and pull up hard on the bar to prevent flipping. Leave enough
room for your crotch to clear the saddle. Then keep your eyes on
the trail and move on—you cleaned it.

Mastering the Whoop-de-do
V-DITCHES ㉖

By John Olsen

One of the most common and challenging obstacles is the ditch. Whether a natural stream bed or man-made for drainage, it involves a steep descent, a sharp transition from downhill to uphill and a steep climb—often with little room at the bottom to switch modes. Ditches can be tricky for the best of riders, and they are the bane of many a novice.

A "V-ditch" is a steep descent, then a steep ascent. The point of the "V" is the point at which the descent and ascent meet. V-ditches require the mastery of a variety of skills, including controlled descending using both brakes, lofting the front wheel and steep climbing using your body's weight to gain traction. You'll also need good eyes and good sense so that before you commit to riding across the black, turgid pool at the bottom of the ditch, you know it's not six feet deep with a mucky bottom. I learned this from experience. Poke with a stick before you leap.

Here's the procedure. As always, with a technical, threatening or scary descent, roll over the edge at walking pace—fast enough to maintain steering, but slow enough to give yourself a chance to control speed on the descent. Keep two fingers on the brake levers as you crest the top, then gently ease the brakes on as you move onto the slope. Use the front brake for most of your speed control and the rear as much as you can without skidding. Keep your weight back as demanded by the steepness of the descent.

The difficulty comes when you get to the bottom. Some ditches are round at their lowest point, which helps the front wheel roll up and onto the climb. But some have sharp down/up transitions or obstacles that can form wheel traps. In these cases you have to help

step
1

Enter the gulch fast enough to maintain steering but slow enough to bail. Control your speed with the front brake.

Keep your weight back and level your pedals. Don't skid the rear wheel. When you come to the transition at the bottom, shift your weight forward, then move your body to the rear sharply while pulling up on the bar. This mini-wheelie puts your front wheel on the up-slope. You might have to try this several times to get it right.

step
2

step
3

Once you're going up, assume the position—the out-of-saddle-climbing position, that is. Keep your head low and forward, your elbows out and pull back on the bar with each downstroke, like you're rowing yourself up the hill.

the front wheel onto the up-slope with body English and timing.

Start with your weight back. Just before the bottom, ease your weight forward. When the front wheel is about one foot away from the transition, move your torso back sharply, pull up on the handlebar and pedal hard. This should pick your front wheel up and land it nicely on the up-slope. If not, dust yourself off, change your timing and try again.

The power application that got your wheel onto the up-slope also signals the beginning of your climbing effort. You must land on the up-slope in your out-of-saddle climbing position: head low, forward and just above the stem and your elbows out. Also be sure that you're pedaling strongly in the right gear. Too low, and you won't be able to execute the wheelie necessary to get your front wheel up; too high, and either the front wheel won't come up, or you won't be able to climb the hill. I suggest your small chainring and third-largest cog. And watch your speed; too much on the decline is a common reason for a rough down/up transition.

Ditches like this require a lot of practice, both because they combine so many skills and because they place such a premium on timing. But they're worth conquering.

HIGH-SPEED ㉗
COMPRESSIONS

By Hank Barlow

You're flying along, smooth and easy, congratulating yourself for your highly developed technique. Suddenly, the trail disappears like morning mist. Before you know it, you're spread-eagled, lying on the ground, wondering what happened.

You hit a compression. And while you flubbed big-time, you discovered yet another opportunity to learn.

A compression is any sudden change in the trail surface that abruptly slams the bike up into your body. Positive compressions are humps where the bike jackhammers you first and then plummets from under your feet, often resulting in unplanned air time. Negative compressions are ditches, erosion gullies and animal wallows—places where your bike suddenly drops from under you then smacks an upslope on the far side. Negative compressions are more common and thus, the subject here.

Compressions come in all sizes, shapes and severity. But there's no need to panic: Once you learn the technique, compressions are easy to handle and, when done well, lots of fun. They're a bit like riding a roller coaster, only on a bike there's no safety bar to keep you aboard. You have to maintain control.

STEPS TO SUCCESS

These basic steps can help you cope with compressions.

1. Watch your speed. The governing factor in managing compressions is speed. The faster you're riding, the greater the impact of the compression. The slower, the less you'll notice it.

While accumulated experience is the only way to know how fast you can hit a compression, you'll rarely be sorry for erring on the side of caution. Consequently, the first tip: Slow before you enter the compression. Lightly apply the brakes. Keep poised above the saddle with your arms and legs flexed, weight slightly back and the crankarms horizontal. Keep your eyes focused on where you're going.

2. Ease the impact. As your front wheel hits the bottom of the depression, anticipate with your arms the impact of the wheel hitting the up-slope. Flex your legs and simultaneously pull up on the handlebar. These motions soften the impact. Again, your eyes should remain focused on the trail ahead.

Your fingers should no longer be on the brake levers. Releasing the brakes is crucial. I've seen many riders panic and squeeze the handlebar for safety as they hit a compression, only to discover (while flying headfirst into the woods) that they forgot their hands were also still on the brake levers.

3. Exhale. Let your body absorb the impact of the sudden transition. Your exhalation (cheeks puffed from breathing out forcefully) should coincide with the absorption. It's as if your torso simply collapses into the bike. In truth, it's the other way around: The bike comes up into your body. Your right leg has also just begun a power stroke to drive the bike up and out of the compression. To maintain traction, pull back with your arms and legs.

You should still be out of the saddle but only slightly. Keep your body low and forward to press down on the front wheel to maintain steering control. As you continue up and out of the compression, simply relax, sit on the saddle and return to your normal upright trail-riding position.

The entire sequence is one smooth, continuous motion. The idea is simply to float your body through the transition in a shallower arc than that taken by the bike. Arms and legs act as shock absorbers. It's easy.

What if your bike has a suspension system? The basic movements don't change, but you won't have to do as much to absorb the compression.

It's a Funky Way to Get Down

SWITCHBACK NOSE WHEELIE ㉘

By John Olsen

Ready to try something a little daring? This move comes in handy when you're riding the Rockies or the mountains farther west, where switchbacks commonly snake down the steep mountainsides. But it has its place in Eastern riding, too—a switchback in the 1994 course for the 24 Hours of Canaan in West Virginia took down many an unsuspecting rider.

This skill uses a phenomenon normally associated with the early moments of an over-the-bar crash: a nose wheelie. By taking advantage of the natural lightness of the rear wheel on a steep descent and combining the right line, a steering move, hop, front brake squeeze and body twist, you can execute a 180-degree turn within the confines of a switchback without sliding and damaging the trail.

The move is potentially dangerous, so rehearse it thoroughly in a place with a safe landing before using it in a high-stakes situation. And wear a helmet and any other protective clothing you have. Loosen or unbuckle both toe straps. You'll have to dab quickly a few times before mastering the turn, so swap your clipless pedals for standard issue until you have it down.

Enter the turn wide, on the high side of the trail. Coast at a walking pace. Test your brakes. Make sure they're working predictably before you drop into the steep part.

You're going to pivot on the front tire, so make room for the rear to swing around by steering into the apex of the corner. Your weight should be slightly (just slightly) rearward. I like to have my inside pedal (the downhill one) back for leverage.

As your front tire reaches the apex of the corner, dig the inside grip down and back and move your torso forward. Pinch the front brake lever firmly and give a little hop with your feet. At this point, your rear wheel should leave the ground (EGAD!). You'll soon know if you've hopped or squeezed too hard. If so, get up and try again.

In midflip, push the inside grip ahead. This twists the rear wheel around the corner. It also tilts the bike away from the abyss, which keeps you from overbalancing and falling to the outside when you land.

Because of your considerable lateral momentum, you need to land the back wheel far enough around the corner so that you don't get "high sided" over the edge. This is one of the trickiest parts of the turn. Once you "stick" the landing, the rest is cake. Just pedal away with a big stupid grin on your face.

What to Do When
You're Riding on the Edge
HILLSIDE TRAVERSE ㉙

By Jay DeJesus

Argh! I'm out riding a fast loop when I drop out of the woods and see a loose, off-camber, narrow, STEEP hillside traverse. The key to crossing successfully is to avoid riding off the edge. (How Zen-like.) Go ahead and laugh. It's been done. Here's how I avoided the big tumble.

step ① Dropping in, I weight the outside pedal and lean the bike away from the hill to avoid hitting the inside pedal. I stand up and keep my nose on the uphill side of the stem. This key move lets me lean my bike out while my body stays centered on the trail.

step ②

As the trail straightens, so do I. The only way I can blow it here is by looking over the edge instead of at the trail ahead.

step ③

Poking around an outcrop of dirt, my head and upper body shift in again to lean my bike outward. In the process, I steer my front wheel wide to help the rear wheel clear the outcrop. This outward lean also puts more of the tire tread on the ground. A "knees-apart" stance gives a momentarily broader platform for balance.

step **4**

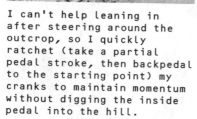

I can't help leaning in after steering around the outcrop, so I quickly ratchet (take a partial pedal stroke, then backpedal to the starting point) my cranks to maintain momentum without digging the inside pedal into the hill.

step **5**

Whoa! I stay as far inside as possible. As I ratchet with my left foot, forcing the rear tire into the hill for more traction, I thrust forward with my arms to finish the section. Whew!

BLOWING UP ㉚

By Joe Kita

May it never happen to you, but if it does, here's a memorable example from 1993 world downhill champ Mike King on how to survive a rear flat at high speed. He was doing about 35 mph at the apex of a right-hand hairpin when his tire popped.

step ① "The first thing you have to be concerned with is balance. In the first photo I'm leaning forward, trying to take weight off the rear wheel, while also extending my left leg, dragging the right and grabbing the front brake. All this is causing me to angle the bike into the slide. It's the scariest point. If the rear wheel had hit a rock, I'd have been airborne."

step 2

"In the second shot, I'm starting to lay the bike down. My weight is shifting more to the middle of the bike, I'm braking more with my right foot and the rear wheel, but my left leg is still pegged. That's important because you need to keep the bike sliding straight downhill."

step 3

"Then, touchdown! I'm going about 15 mph in the third shot, and I was very grateful I was wearing knee guards. Most of my weight is on my knee, and my left leg is still clipped into the pedal and still straight, guiding the bike away from me."

step
4

"Right after it was over I was extremely bummed, but then I was
just thankful to be alive.... Know your limits, wear safety gear,
but consider me real lucky."

STAIR MEISTER ㉛

By Hans Rey, as told to Scott Martin

You may never be able to (or want to) ride your mountain bike off cliffs or over cars like trials master Hans Rey. But wouldn't it be nice to learn some basic moves to improve your trail-riding skills or just amaze your friends? That's what I thought. Here are Rey's best tips for mastering riding down stairs.

Note: If you can find wooden stairs (as opposed to concrete), you'll save a lot of skin. To practice, head to a park that has walking trails (provided it's legal to ride there). These trails often have wooden steps built into steep terrain. If there are no stairs on your riding routes, these skills can be used on any bumpy descent, particularly dry streambeds, where water erosion often creates "steps."

- First go down a curb, then try stairs with two or three steps.
- Stand and keep your weight back.
- Keep your pedals horizontal, with your "chocolate foot" (your strongest foot) forward.
- Keep your handlebar straight. Grip the bar tightly but let your upper body absorb shock.
- Keep your wheels perpendicular to the stairs.
- Go as slowly as possible without losing balance.
- Be committed. Don't hesitate.
- It's okay to brake, but use the front brake with finesse.

If you use click-in pedals, keep the tension loose and remember to click out early if you get in trouble.

Hans Rey's tip for successful stair-riding: Keep your
strongest foot forward.

Part 4 Dealing with the

Elements

ROLLING OVER ROCKS ③②

By Hank Barlow

For me, there's no more forbidding terrain than a rock field. I've never had to cross a minefield, but that's what comes to mind when the trail turns to a jagged sea of stone. Every serrated edge in my path, every angled ledge and all fist-size rocks conjure images of broken bones and blood. Cleaning such a section isn't my first goal; surviving it is.

On a trail through a meadow of wildflowers, bailing out is never a problem. I hardly give it a thought. But jumping or falling off a bike in a rock field can be disastrous. Spraining an ankle, cracking a wrist, separating a shoulder or demolishing a rear derailleur are possible, painful outcomes.

No wonder rock fields are intimidating. It's important to be careful, but if you're thinking of crashing, you probably will. To master the craggy sections, the trick is to think of them as the most wonderful challenges, as stages on which to use those skills you've been arduously honing.

There is only one way to enter a rock field: aggressively. But attack with controlled passion and don't think of the rocks as an enemy. Look at the passage as a dance, and you and your bike as partners following a melody.

Like any dance, you'll need to get off your butt. Riding a rock field requires every shock-absorbing advantage that your arms and legs can provide. An out-of-saddle position also gives you more confidence to ride with power and conviction—like a warrior. When standing, balance your weight on the balls of your feet. Flex your knees, grip the handlebar firmly and focus your eyes on the path ahead.

Don't shift into an extremely low gear. You want to feel resistance when pedaling. You might also want to place one finger on each brake lever. A timely trackstand can be the difference between walking and riding.

USE YOUR MOMENTUM

The line you pick is important: Look where you want to go, not where you don't. Be prepared to improvise when the desired path doesn't work. In rocky sections this happens frequently. But don't dwell on finding the "right" line. It's more important to keep moving. Momentum is a powerful force that can propel you over rough stuff that even an expert's finesse won't dent.

Don't give up. Stay on the bike as long as you can. This is when those trackstands come in handy. Rather than reaching for the security of the ground with one foot the moment you expect to stall, balance for a moment and study the situation, then drive your bike forward with a powerful thrust. You'll be amazed at how often you can ride a section you had gauged as hopeless.

I first discovered this years ago while climbing Pearl Pass in Colorado. About a third of the way up the Aspen side, the roadbed becomes a nightmare. I took one look at the water-splashed rocks and knew there was no way I'd clean it. But this was also a day when I was feeling confident. So I attacked, keeping my weight balanced, pedaling aggressively and concentrating on a line of least resistance. I was so consumed in my effort that I somehow pedaled well beyond my expectations.

Then I reached a nasty section that offered no escape. The line that might lead me out of the crags had disappeared. But I was still inspired. Instead of quitting and dabbing, I balanced for a moment, then drove the bike straight through the jumble of rocks. Not only did I escape, but my momentum carried me through the passage. I succeeded by keeping my feet in the clips until the last possible moment.

LEAN AND CLEAN

While balance and momentum are keys to cleaning a rock field, pedal clearance is often a tricky snag. I guarantee you'll smack a pedal on a rock more often than you want, but the result doesn't have to be catastrophic. When you hit one, remain out of the saddle and immediately lean away from the rock. This often raises the pedal to clear the obstacle. Another way is to let the bike bounce. This will work as long as you keep your feet in the clips and hands on the bar to maintain control.

Eventually, you'll sense where your pedals are and know when clearance is adequate and when it isn't. If the passage is particularly narrow, try half-pedal strokes until you're through. (With your pedals on the level, pedal forward half a revolution, then ratchet them back.) Half-pedaling feels awkward at first but it works, particularly if you select a slightly higher gear. In a very low one, you probably won't generate enough forward motion.

Sometimes, pedal clearance is solved by riding over rocks instead of slipping around them. To do this, simultaneously pull up on the handlebar and drive the bike forward with a powerful pedal stroke—but just a quick one. Don't worry about the back wheel; it'll follow. Remember, this isn't a wheelie. You only want to ease the front wheel over the rock. Once you've accomplished this, pedal clearance shouldn't be a problem.

Always be wary of rounded, fist-size rocks that aren't embedded in the trail. They're hazardous. The moment a tire rolls onto one, the rock spits to one side, usually rudely dumping the rider. Aim for the small rocks or the big ones. The small stuff is ridable, and larger rocks won't move. Be leery of rocks covered with lichen or moss. If they're wet, they're very slippery.

One important caution: While it's necessary to be aggressive, always ride under control. Rock fields are dangerous and unforgiving. The farther you are from civilization, the more cautious you should be. Listen to yourself. If you don't feel like attempting a section, get off and portage. The rock field will always be there. Tackle it on a day when you're strong and confident.

A Guide to Ridin' in the Rain

WET AND DIALED 33

By Hank Barlow

Riding a mountain bike is a matter of balance—fore, aft, lateral and mental. A rider maintains stability with body English. On a warm, sunny day when the trail is dry and firm, riding becomes laughably easy. But when the weather turns nasty and wet, suddenly we're confronted with a new set of challenges. Most riders respond by staying indoors and reading books or repairing their bikes. But by doing so they miss what can be one of cycling's most exhilarating and beautiful experiences.

Of course, there is one valid reason to stay indoors, and that's when trails are too wet to be ridden without creating erosive ruts. On those days, reading and working on your bike are appropriate options. A day off won't hurt you, but it will help the trails.

The key to enjoyable rain riding is preparation. Start with a nourishing breakfast, such as oatmeal or whole-grain pancakes, which will keep you going through hours of exertion. Dry cereal won't suffice. Pack plenty of food for the ride and make sure it stays dry and within easy reach. Energy bars are particularly effective. During the ride, drink water and nibble often—at least once every 20 to 30 minutes—to replenish energy stores and maintain a strong attitude.

Dress to stay warm and dry, from a hooded visor to booties. For undergarments, choose fabrics that provide insulation when wet, such as wool or polypropylene. Don't wear cotton next to your skin.

Your outer layer must be waterproof, not simply water resistant. There's a considerable difference. I mention this from experience with friends from California, who tried to stay dry by donning windbreakers during a snow shower in the Rockies above Crested Butte. Their flimsy outerwear was useless. By waterproof, I mean a jacket and pants made from Gore-Tex or another fabric that prevents water from penetrating.

Yes, you'll still get wet from sweat and condensation even when you're wearing breathable, waterproof garments. But with the proper clothing underneath, you'll remain comfortable. In addition to keeping the rain out, waterproof clothing is also the best protection against the cooling effect of wind.

SMOOTH AND LIGHT

Okay, you've eaten, you're properly dressed and you're ready to ride. Now all you have to do is stay centered on the bike. Maintaining balance between front and rear wheels is more critical on a wet trail than on a dry one. Traction diminishes and can become unreliable. One moment your tires are biting with a sure grip and the next they're sliding. You have to learn to read the ground, to get a feel for its changing conditions.

Go slow. Speed creates forces in the wet that can turn disastrous in a moment. Strive for maximum smoothness. Ride as if you're flowing over the trail. When you first apply the brakes and they seem to slip, don't panic. After a few revolutions, friction will dry the braking surfaces. Remember, if you're squeezing the levers to the max, the pads will suddenly grab hard. So be prepared to lighten the lever pressure when this happens. Feathering the pads against the rims just before hard braking can smooth this transition.

Watch for roots and branches on the trail. Roots are especially slippery. When approaching one, reduce speed, ride over it at a right angle and never apply the front brake—this will cause the wheel to skitter. The rear wheel shouldn't cause a problem, as long as you don't try to accelerate while your back tire is still on the root. When it's impossible to cross the root at a right angle, gently hop the front wheel, then be ready for the back tire to slip sideways as it hits.

Climbing in wet conditions usually requires a little more weight on the rear wheel. Maintain a smooth and even pedaling pressure for optimum traction. If the rear wheel slips, shift more weight back and keep going.

Descending on a wet trail can be tricky because it's easy to lock your brakes. But don't stop using the front brake; just apply it with more finesse, shift your weight rearward and keep the front wheel pointed straight.

If the front wheel starts to skid, release the front brake and apply more force to the rear lever. A skidding rear wheel is easier to control, but it will often damage the trail. Feather the brake to avoid skidding and always slow before you descend a steep slope.

Wooden bridges are particularly slippery in wet weather. They can usually be crossed safely if you approach them straight on, but be wary even when you're safely on board. The slightest mismove can cause you to slide out. If you have to approach the bridge at an angle, get off and walk your bike. It's not worth landing in the drink and dealing with wet shoes and clothing, particularly if you're still far from home.

Anticipation is another key to riding in the rain. Give yourself lots of leeway for the unknown. If the trail is buried in autumn foliage, for example, reduce your speed and be prepared for broken branches or roots that you may never notice until you hit them. This doesn't mean riding in constant fear. Simply give yourself enough margin for error to deal with the unexpected, such as a moss-covered rock slathered with wet leaves, the sudden collapse of a water-soaked trail above a mole's tunnel or the distraction of a brilliant rainbow dancing in your peripheral vision.

DIRTY LITTLE SECRETS ③④

By John Olsen

I live in mud. I eat it for breakfast, lunch and dinner. I ride in mud for nine months out of the year. Not bottomless midwestern river-bottom mud, but good, honest, wet-forest loam a few inches thick atop a good gravel-and-clay base. It's slippery, but it's neither impassable nor environmentally sensitive.

Based on my years in the mire, here are ten riding and equipment tips on how to deal with mud, assuming that your riding area is made up of the right geological mix and that mud riding is a reasonable thing to do. Remember: Screw up, close a trail . . . .

1. Nip slicks in the bud. Get a rear tire that won't plug up and become a de facto slick. Most will, especially tires with forward-facing scoops or wide, straight-across tread blocks. The best mud tire I've found is the Specialized Storm Control, either the 1.8-inch or 2.2-inch version. It almost never plugs. For the front, where plugging is less of a concern, I like Panaracer Darts or Smokes. In any case, use a low pressure—not so low that you get pinch flats, but almost that low—to lessen the chances of crashes on slippery roots and rocks.

2. Lube liberally. Muddy water washes the lube from the chain, which leads to chainsuck, so lube your chain before and after every ride with a good wet-weather product. I use Tri-Flow with an Allsop applicator (a blessing from the gods of wet weather), but there are other good chain lubes out there. I go through it by the gallon.

3. Change your brake pads. They'll need work after almost every ride in the mud.

4. Don't negelct your cables. Buy cables in bulk and replace them frequently. I change critical cables about once every two months,

When you're slogging through the mud, you need a plug-resistant rear tire.

with several cleanings in between. Headsets, bottom brackets, hubs and freewheels all die young when immersed in dirty water. Be prepared to work on these components frequently and budget for their replacement. As for your postride bike wash, use only a low pressure hose or soapy brush and keep the water stream well away from all seals and bearings.

5. Stay on your saddle. I love to stand up, but doing so doesn't work in muck—you need to keep that rear wheel loaded at all times.

6. Stop slips before they start. Run one gear higher than you would in the dry. This reduces torque to the back wheel, and you will slip less.

7. Drag your brakes before you need them. This cleans your rims for serious braking.

8. Think before you charge. Watch for strangely smooth, level, matte-finished surfaces on the trail—especially if they bubble. Such surfaces usually hide a collection of fine silt, washed into a low spot by the rains. These muck ponds can be deep and energy swallowing. If you're not sure, send some eager young rider ahead as a depth probe. This is why we breed teenagers, after all.

9. Watch those puddles. Don't charge into a potentially deep puddle if you don't know the terrain intimately. I have watched riders disappear completely (except for bubbles) in deep puddles. Fortunately, these riders were either tall or could swim, but we all got wet pulling their bikes out.

10. Learn to read the terrain. Mud riding is fun in a perverse kind of way, but not everybody should do it. If your bike is going to permanently mar or damage the trail, stay off it! It all depends on where you are and on the soil and slope you are riding on. Basically, if the mud is so bad that riding is a pain, you probably shouldn't be riding it. If you're leaving tracks (other than in low-spot mud-gathering places), you probably shouldn't be riding it. If water is running down the tracks you leave, you definitely shouldn't be doing it. If your tracks will be frozen into adobe until the next rain (and maybe the next decade), you absolutely shouldn't be doing it.

SNOW JOB ㉟

By Captain Dondo With Tim Blumenthal

Some narrow-minded, nonsnowbelt dwellers might think that winter weather is reason enough to limit your mountain bike riding. *Au contraire.* When else can you ride otherwise mucky trails (with a clean bike and conscience), cavort through swamps and pedal across lakes? Even the famed Iditarod sled-dog trail, home of the 200-mile Iditasport mountain bike/cross-country ski/snowshoe race, is nothing but muskeg swamps, lakes and mud flats during summer. Snow and ice make it ridable.

Cold weather brings at least as many different kinds of winter riding surfaces as summer. Each requires a degree of forethought and finesse to negotiate. But overall, snow and ice riding is less technical than summer singletrack, so don't be afraid to try it. Here are the most common winter conditions and some tips for enjoying them.

Hardpack (crust). Winter's answer to slickrock. When the top layer of snow hardens from wind or refreezing, you can ride it virtually anywhere. The thing about crust is it will hold you up long enough to gain your complete trust, then catch you unaware as the front wheel punches through and you do a layout gainer over the handlebar. For that reason, always scoot your butt way back when descending—and make sure your helmet is on tight. The firmest crust forms after sunset and stays that way until just after sunrise. Full moon nights and early morning are the best times for riding it. It's easy to get carried away having fun, but try not to get caught too far from home when it softens. A fast 2-hour ride out can turn into a hellish 12-hour hike back if you're not paying attention.

Light, dry powder. Fun to ride through fast because it sprays up and

Snow skills aren't too technical. But look out for
hidden obstacles that can turn you into a snow angel.

leaves a wake behind you. But be careful of solid objects lurking
below the surface, especially if you're running lower tire pressure
for better flotation. Smacking a log or rock could pinch and puncture the tube. Powder also has a knack for jamming chains, so be
sure to lube your chain. As with sand in summer, deeper, heavier
and wetter powder requires more power to plow through. Keep
your shoulders and hips loose and let the bike move beneath you.
Snow may be solid, but balance is fluid.

    Ice. About the only strategy is to try to survive. Technique isn't
much of an issue—studded tires and falling down are. For safety,
avoid places where ice may be unpredictable, such as inlets or out-
lets on lakes and ponds. Also avoid river ice almost anywhere but

CHOOSING YOUR TRAIL

Unless you live in Corpus Christi, Texas, or the Florida Keys, you can probably find snow-covered trails in the winter months within a day's drive. It may be a long day, but what the heck, it's the off-season, right? Here are a few places to look—and avoid.

○ Trails packed by snowmobiles are ideal because they generally provide a reliably smooth, hard surface. They're usually wide enough for comfort and rarely too steep for traction. Also, if you have an accident or a back-country breakdown, assistance may come motoring along just when you need it.

○ Groomed cross-country ski trails can be excellent, but they shouldn't be ridden without permission. Stay off soft trails because fat tires can damage the surface and make them less ski-able.

○ Mountain bike trails, the paths you normally ride, are obvious picks. But mild grades that are easy in summer are generally too steep for winter riding. And if the snow is deep but not packed, forget it.

○ Rails-to-trails conversions can be outstanding snow rides. Their grades are mild, they're wide and easily packed and parking and access are rarely problems.

○ Well-frozen lakes covered by a few inches of crusted snow can be fun. Just be sure the ice is thick and be aware that wind can blow away the snow and your chances of staying upright.

○ Deep unpacked snow, unless it's featherweight powder atop a firm base, is a beast. Wheels sink and the ride stinks.

○ Slush. Mush. Enough said?

Overall, snow riding demands a keen sense of weather and topography. Surface conditions often change quickly. Trails with a northern exposure are less vulnerable to sun and warm winds and generally offer more consistent surface conditions. The flip side, of course, is that they're colder. The higher the elevation, the better the chance of finding adequate snow conditions. This is particularly relevant to eastern riding. In the Rockies and west, super-high elevations often present avalanche danger and wildly variable weather conditions.

Alaska. If you have to get off and push on an ice-covered trail, it's best to have a few sheet-metal screws embedded in your boot soles. Otherwise, you're in for a walk on the wild slide.

Slush. Almost ice, but never ride through it. Always portage around. Slush sprayed on a freewheel is the recipe for a mountain bike snow cone. It looks neat, but you can't pedal it.

A TRICK TO TAKE YOU DOWN

In almost any kind of snow, descents require a special technique. Crystals accumulate between the brake pads and rims, so your brakes may not work when you need them. Test them far in advance. Sometimes they'll wipe clean, but other times you'll have to employ the "Iditaskid"—a strange thing discovered in the midnight sun by the men and women who moil for Iditasport gold.

Slide your buns onto the top tube. With one foot on the pedal, dip the other foot into the snow as an auxiliary brake/outrigger/curb feeler. Keep the braking knee slightly bent so you can make minor adjustments for terrain variations. With practice, you can Iditaskid in complete control down nearly anything. Just don't expect to do it slowly.

AFTER THE ICEMAN COMETH

You're back from riding in a winter wonderland and your bike is caked with ice and frozen mud. Here are some quick cleaning tips to do before running for that hot cup of cocoa.

◉ Melt the goo by pouring buckets of warm water over the frozen parts. Pay particular attention to the cog, derailleur and bottom bracket areas.

◉ Wipe the moisture off with an old bath towel and leave your bike in a warm room to dry completely.

◉ Lube the chain, cables and derailleurs and inject grease into all the appropriate ports.

Your bike is now dry, protected from corrosion and ready to roll some more.

OVERCOMING ALTITUDE ㊱

By Scott Martin

D on't trust anyone under 5,000 feet"—T-shirt *slogan seen at the Mountain Bike National Championships in Mammoth, California (elevation 9,000 feet).*

From the Sierra Nevada Mountain Metric Century in California to Fat Tire Bike Week in the Colorado Rockies, mountain bikers know the delights of high-altitude pedaling—spectacular scenery, challenging terrain and laid-back good times. But sea-level riders who head for the mountains also experience another revelation: Their fitness literally vanishes into thin air.

If you plan to be ridin' high on a cycling vacation this year, take time now to scan our tips on pedaling at altitude. They'll help you adapt quicker, recover faster and avoid such nasty side effects as headache, nausea and insomnia.

First, though, some background on the high ground. The reason it's harder to breathe at altitude isn't that there's less oxygen in the air. Rather, there's less barometric pressure forcing air into your lungs. To deliver enough oxygenated blood to working muscles, you must breathe faster and your heart has to pump more rapidly.

If you live near sea level, you probably won't notice any difference until you ascend above 5,000 feet. Studies of elite athletes show a significant 6 to 8 percent decrease in oxygen uptake at about 6,000 feet, according to Jay T. Kearney, Ph.D., director of sports science for the U.S. Olympic Committee. And at about 8,000 feet, you should be wary of acute mountain sickness (AMS).

The symptoms of AMS include headache, shortness of breath when exercising, insomnia, fatigue, irritability, decreased appetite, nausea and vomiting. These can appear as soon as four to six hours

RULES UPON ARRIVAL

Here's what experts have to say about dealing with the effects of altitude.

1. Don't take chances. If you experience AMS (acute mountain sickness) symptoms, stop riding. If severe, go to a lower altitude.

2. Go easy on the alcohol. Not only will alcohol (and coffee and soda with caffeine) further dehydrate you by increasing urination, says Ed Burke, Ph.D., exercise physiologist in Colorado Springs, but "alcoholic beverages have roughly twice the effect at elevation than at sea level." This may sound like fun when you're hanging out at the bar in the evening, but it's not so enjoyable when you're hanging over your 'bar the next morning.

3. Drink lots of water. The air is drier at altitude, so you dehydrate quicker. Sweat also evaporates faster, so it's harder to tell that you're losing water.

4. Eat more carbs, less protein. "A general carbohydrate diet and a decrease in the amount of protein ingested will lighten the load on your body as it works to restore a comfortable physiological balance," says Dr. Burke. Why? You can store more fluid in your body with carbohydrates, and it takes less oxygen to burn carbs at altitude.

5. Ride high, sleep low. If you have trouble sleeping at altitude, spend the night at a lower elevation than where you're riding. A drop of as little as 1,000 feet can be enough to help you breathe easier.

6. Block the sun. Solar radiation is greater at elevation, so wear sunscreen, sunglasses and light-colored clothing. If possible, avoid riding from 10:00 A.M. to 2:00 P.M.

7. Dress smart. The weather can change swiftly at altitude, so take warm, water-repellent clothing to ward off hypothermia. And remember that for every 1,000 feet you gain, the temperature drops 3.5°F.

after reaching 8,000 feet. They're most severe on the second and third days and usually disappear by the fourth day. The only sure cure is to descend, although mild symptoms can be treated by going to bed and drinking lots of fluids.

Ironically, the physically fit are more likely to get AMS than sedentary people. "The more fit you are, the more susceptible you are because you tend to push yourself harder," says Ed Burke, Ph.D., exercise physiologist in Colorado Springs (elevation 6,000 ft.).

Supporting his assertion is a 1988 study of U.S. Cycling Federation members who were competing in races held above 5,000 feet. Researchers found that 25 percent of the 1,500 riders had signs of AMS, although only 3.4 percent suffered moderate rather than mild cases.

THINKING AHEAD

The best way to prepare for high-elevation cycling is to make your body as efficient as possible by training harder than you would for a similar ride at sea level.

"A lot of people come to Fat Tire Bike Week thinking they're fit, but they find out they're not," says Don Cook, a former off-road racer who lives at 8,900 feet in Crested Butte, Colorado, home of the annual festival. "You need to get in a lot of good, solid climbing miles and do some anaerobic stuff." (Anaerobic means "without oxygen"—in other words, very intense exercise.)

Even if you're not a superpowered cyclist, though, you can perform well and stay healthy by getting reasonably fit and planning your trip carefully. Dr. Kearney says that ideally, you should have 10 to 14 days to acclimatize. The classic way is to ascend gradually, spending a day or more at intermediate altitudes. If you're going to Crested Butte, for instance, you might fly into Denver and spend a couple of days in the Mile-High City before climbing to your mile-and-a-half-high destination. If you're going even higher—10,000 to 14,000 feet—experts recommend ascending 1,000 feet per day.

But don't despair if you don't have enough time to slowly acclimatize. Experts such as Dr. Kearney also say that you can perform well with a blitzkrieg approach—doing your hardest riding as soon as you arrive at altitude. This can work if you're focusing on a race or special long ride.

"There are all sorts of opinions," says Cook, "but I know from experience that people who come up here are better off getting in their licks during the first few days." That's because it takes about 24 to 48 hours before the effects of altitude take hold, explains Dr. Burke.

After going hard initially, Cook recommends resting on the third or fourth day as your body adapts. "When my buddies come up from Marin County, they're at their best the first couple of days," Cook explains. "Then all of a sudden they're walking up stairs, and it hits them."

After six or seven days, Cook says you begin to rally. If you're fortunate enough to be on a two-week vacation, you'll probably start feeling strong the last few days.

Dr. Kearney says this process is similar to what your body encounters in training. Like hard riding, pedaling at altitude is exhaustive and debilitating in the short term, but with proper recovery, you get stronger.

To be competitive with cyclists who live at altitude, though, you need to spend more time there. The reason is that it takes several weeks for the number of oxygen-carrying red blood cells to increase.

Getting completely acclimatized takes even longer. "There's this continual process of adaptation—of red blood cells increasing—and that takes many months," says Dr. Burke. "But adaptation rates are individual."

Learning Where to Set Your Sights

TRAIL READING 37

By Geoff Drake

Looking ahead is critical in mountain biking. You must consider all your options in half a second, and a good rider will pick the right one. This is called sight-reading, and it's one reason that John Tomac, 1994 NORBA downhill champion, can fly down a trail he's never ridden before. He reads the trail better than the average rider.

Look up the trail and see what's ahead. Is there a rut to avoid or a better line to take? Remember that the path that looks easy now may lead you right to that large rock up ahead, while the harder but still ridable line to the left will lead you safely past it.

You may think you're only saving seconds with good trail reading (after all, you can ride around that rock), but those seconds add up, and the pros know it can take less than a second to win (or lose) a race. Be constantly aware, and you'll be more likely to lead the pack.

PRO TRAIL-READING TIPS

Following are riding tips used by pro riders from the Specialized/2-Calorie Quest team and a quick drill you can do to build your skills.

Silvia Furst, 1992 cross-country world champion. Furst suggests you think of your eyes like a camera, taking a picture of what's ahead, then what's right in front. Record what you see.

Peter Swenson, Specialized pro. Swenson says that people tend to just look at their front wheel or the wheel ahead of them. They might know what's in the immediate corner, but not that it's followed by a short, steep ascent that requires a downshift. Look up the trail and look through the bike ahead of you so you don't get stuck behind someone.

Golden Brainard, *Specialized pro.* Brainard suggests that sometime in training, you stop your bike and read the terrain ahead. See what clues there are to help you ride that section. Is there a rut or some sand to avoid? Train your focus to switch back and forth, near and far. Think of it like looking up while you're driving, then down at your speedometer. Constantly go back and forth.

TRAIL-READING DRILL

Practice looking up to a spot 20 to 30 yards ahead and then down in front of your wheel. The more you do this, the better you become at it. Pick a section and exaggerate this—be constantly scanning. As you get better at trail reading, practice on increasingly steeper descents. This will force you to quicken your scanning ability and teach you to pick out the most important obstacles to avoid.

MOONLIGHT RAMBLE ③⑧

By Bill Strickland

What I remember best about my first night ride was not riding. There were other parts that sizzled my senses: how this wobbling bubble of light and frantic activity you're pedaling in slides against a darkness that stands as solid and unmoving as a wall; how the silence of light-shy animals and insects rolls out in front of you like a wave and lingers behind like a ship's wake; and how sometimes your addled brain begins to believe there's no ground at all except the small strip in front of your wheel and that if you fall, you fall off the earth. Really.

But what sticks with me most vividly is stopping for water—and the aftermath. My wife, Beth, and I had ascended singletrack to a plateau about halfway up the wooded ridge of our local playground, South Mountain. We sat in our little island of light, drinking water and looking out at the night and feeling, I think, somewhat adventurous but secure. Then she clicked off one of her handlebar-mounted headlights. So did I. Then another, and another. Click, click, click, click, click—darkness.

We hadn't planned this impromptu blackout. It just happened. And although I'm usually not too much of a chicken, it scared me. Maybe it was because suddenly we had left our bubble and were part of the dark unknown. Or maybe I allowed myself so much fear because I knew there was no real danger. I could enjoy it. I could ride it like a mountain bike.

Prophetic words. Because after Beth and I switched our lights on and laughed ourselves back to sanity, we held onto the fear we'd found and spun it out all the way back down the mountain. It gave us a rush we hadn't ridden with before, an edge that sharpened the wavery view of the trail and illuminated the turns and obstacles that at night leap unexpectedly into your path like living things. We were so on top of our adrenaline that when two of our lights faded we picked up the pace.

Even though the experience lasted maybe 15 minutes on trails that I've ridden a hundred times, those moments were some of the sweetest of my short mountain biking life.

NIGHT LIFE

I've chased that fantastic feeling on other nights, but have never caught it again. Even so, I've become an avowed nocturnal knobber. I agree (although for different reasons) with the old wisdom of witches, warlocks and other nasty types: The night has things to teach you. Especially us beginners. Even if you don't fall into the unthinking groove of perfection, you are forced to ride more instinctively and reactively than you do in daylight.

In typical sunlit conditions, novices should try to scan about 30 to 40 feet ahead. (Sometimes even farther—up to 100 feet when you're cooking along a smooth, open downhill, for instance.) This gives you time to anticipate trail conditions. You have time to search the trail for the best line. You're able to set up—and psych up—for tough moves.

You can't do that at night. Some of the best bike lights may throw beams that far, but they can't replace the full-on illumination of that big yellow skyball. No matter what light you're using, after sundown, stuff sneaks into your path and surprises you.

It's a second-by-second test of your skill. Can you pull a wheelie from a near standstill? Muscle your rear wheel over a rip in the earth?

Ride at night and you'll find out. If you're like me, you'll dab (stop and put a foot down) more than you clean (ride over obstacles without stopping). But you'll do more than you thought you could. While you're trying, you'll be honing your handling skills and balance, training your eyes and brains to pick up and process more trail information more quickly and developing an instant-react mode that could prevent an emergency some sunny day.

Enough rationalization, though. These benefits are nice, but the real reason to night ride is for fun. Night riding is strange, it's different and it's another way to break out of the grid, which is what mountain biking is all about. "Normal" people don't ride at night. Thank God.

CREATURES OF THE DARK

Sounds cool huh? But also a little intimidating. At least that's how I felt. Like most mountain biking stuff, though, night riding is a little harder than it sounds but not as hard as you think it'll be.

Here are five tips to help you ride safely off into the sunset.

1. Don't be an idiot. For your first ride, pick a trail you know and ride slower than you think you should until you get used to the sensation. Ready to speed up? Don't. Wait until that first obstacle or blind turn pops up and tosses you off your bike. While you're on the ground contemplating your owie, think how much worse it would hurt if you'd been flying. Now you're ready to find your personal speed limit.

2. Do the light thing. Those high-tech lighting systems make night riding safer and more fun, but don't delay your first ride if all you have on hand are cheap lights. Hang enough lousy illuminators on your handlebar, and you'll get adequate night sight.

Whatever you use, make sure the beams are solid for at least five feet in front of your wheel and provide some illumination for at least ten feet. And carry a small emergency-only light in your jersey pocket or saddle bag. It'll come in handy when you biff your others.

Also remember that unless you're using a helmet-mounted light, you have to point your handlebar wherever you want to look. This takes some getting used to.

3. Hang loose. At night it's more important than ever to relax and just let the trail happen. Instead of trying to force your bike to go a certain way, concentrate on getting over (around, through, under . . .) what the trail puts in front of you. It's a subtle but important difference. A big part of accomplishing this is keeping yourself in the classic "ready" position—elbows and knees loosely bent, butt slightly off the saddle—so you can absorb bumps and control your bike with side-to-side weight shifts.

4. Follow someone. It's amazing how much easier this makes things. Even if all you can see is a dim white spot threading the woods 50 feet ahead of you, you'll have a general idea of where the trail goes. It's one less info bit that your overworked brain will have to absorb.

5. Follow the moon. That is, try to ride when luna is bright. Most of us are so daylight-oriented that we think of the night as the night. Dark is dark. But riding beneath a silver sliver and beneath a full moon are two completely different eyesight experiences. In fact, longtime lunatics tell me that full moons can be bright enough for riding without artificial lights. I believe 'em. I think I'll wait a while before trying, though.

Part 5 Tips from the

Pros

OBSTACLE COURSE ㊴

By the <u>Mountain Bike</u> and <u>Bicycling</u> Staffs

You're cruising along the trail, gaining confidence with each pedal stroke, when your sights fall on a four-inch-high log in your path. You can either stop and hike-a-bike over, or you can bust a move and clean the obstacle. Here's how.

GETTING OVER: EXPERT ADVICE

These tips from the pros can help you make it over any obstacle with confidence. (Use the skill-building drill before heading for the trail.)

Tom Hillard, Specialized coach. "So many riders coming from the road are stiff and don't move around on their bikes. Use your body weight to lunge up and over things. The first thing is to get your front wheel over. To do this, you can simply yank on the handlebar, but that makes it hard to control how high the front end comes up. You can also pedal hard in a low gear. And with a suspension fork, you can push down and allow the rebound to raise the wheel. For most riders the best way is a combination: pushing on the pedals and pulling up on the bar at the same time.

"To get the back wheel over, pull the front wheel up as you abruptly push the bar forward. This causes the front end to drop and the back to rise. The other way is to pull up on the toe clips while in a standing position."

Wayne Croasdale, Specialized pro. "Everyone has a stronger leg—the one you kick a ball with. Try to have that leg set up to apply pressure and get up and over an obstacle. Also, use a lot of upper-body motion. When your front wheel is midway over an obstacle, use your toe clips to lift the back wheel over. Your weight will be back, and then it will be thrown forward like a dolphin arcing through the water. You can also use one obstacle as a jump to get over the next one, such as when a one-foot bump is followed by a small rock."

Ned Overend, six-time NORBA national champion and pro mountain bike racer and coach. "Sometimes you need to use a "stutter step" so your pedal doesn't hit a small obstacle. This means only taking the pedal halfway down, then lifting it back up to ensure clearance, and pushing down again. Also, sometimes you need to surge just before the obstacle so you have the momentum to go over it. You don't want to apply hard pedal pressure while you're on the obstacle because your rear wheel might break loose."

Ruthie Matthes, 1992 World Cup champion. "My nemesis is log-hopping. I think it comes from a really bad road crash I had (in the Coors Classic) when I slammed into a curb. But the suspension stem on my mountain bike has helped because I can load it up and it springs back, which assists in getting over obstacles. Get your weight back as you approach the object and unweight the front wheel to get it up, then move your weight forward to get the rear end up without slamming into the object. Doing it all quickly is important, too. I start by hopping small sticks, then I try jumping bigger and bigger ones. It's a confidence thing."

David Wiens, 1993 NORBA national champion. "Here's the perfect position for cleaning washboard bumps. Keep your butt above the saddle and weight slightly back. This is a versatile stance; you can rise higher and pedal for a quick burst of speed, or drop quickly back onto your seat."

OBSTACLE DRILL

Place two pairs of cones a few feet apart. Elevate your front wheel when you pass through the first pair and make it land at the second pair to practice controlling the amount of time the wheel is in the air. Or place a small rock or board on the ground, and elevate your front wheel just enough to graze it.

To Everything Turn, Turn, Turn
TWISTING AND TURNING ④⓪

By the <u>Mountain Bike</u> and <u>Bicycling</u> Staffs

Cornering can offer free speed if you do it right. According to Specialized coach Tom Hillard, there are three ways to position your body, as well as three lines you can take through a corner. That's a lot of combinations, but most people only know one. They tend instinctively to go into the corner way too soon and lean as if they're on a road bike. With this method you push your outside pedal down and countersteer by pushing the inside of the handlebar, "carving" the turn. It's fast, but on a mountain bike you risk losing traction and sliding out.

In many cases a better way is what Hillard calls the survival turn. Your weight is to the inside and your bike is upright. It's a good method if you don't know the corner, or if it's slippery and you need control. But it can be slower.

Yet another method is for sand. Normally, if you keep your bike upright, you have to turn the handlebar more. But if you turn your bar in the sand, you'll wash out. Instead, turn it a minimal amount, leaning the bike underneath you while keeping your body upright. Use this anytime you don't want your front wheel to dig in.

Your line through a corner depends on where you make the apex (turning point). A "mid-apex" turn yields the highest average speed by creating a gentle arc and using every bit of the fire road. An "early-apex" turn involves making the actual corner early, then powering out. The idea is to get the turn done and extend the straightaway coming out so you can go faster there. With a "late-apex" turn you dive into the corner and do your actual turning later, extending the straightaway going into it. This means you can brake later and possibly pass someone going in. But you'll be slower coming out.

Missy Giove is a former ski racer who thrives in the fast lane and stays off the brakes.

GOING APEX

To see how the pros deal with making turns, check out the following tips.

Silvia Furst, 1992 cross-country world champion. "I like to put my weight to the inside and pedal through corners. It's like applying the gas in a car as you go around a curve—it helps maintain traction."

Missy Giove, 1994 downhill world champion. "You may not have the skill or experience to risk putting a foot down at 45 mph, but at slower speeds an outrigged limb can help you through a sharp turn. Almost as much as the foot, it's the low and wide stance that will keep you upright and on course."

Jeff Osguthorpe, Specialized pro. "I like the early-apex turn so I can get the corner done with. If you go for the late apex, you'll almost always have to dump a lot of speed coming out."

Juli Furtado, 1995 World Cup champion. "Round your turns in a smooth arc to maintain momentum. Don't zigzag. Lean your body more than your bike to speed your way through abrupt changes in direction."

Wayne Croasdale, Specialized pro. "The main thing is to come out of the corner fast. So I like to 'pre-turn' (early apex). This means I can come out fast, in a straight line."

Jason McRoy, 1993 British downhill champion. "I put the emphasis on getting my weight on the outside pedal. A lot of people put their outside pedal down, but they really don't push on it. I put a lot of weight on it and carve the turn."

THE DRILL

Try using an early-, mid- and late-apex turn in the same corner to see the advantages and disadvantages of each. Use cones to mark the turning point.

STOP RIGHT THERE ㊶

By the <u>Bicycling</u> Staff

Knowing how to use your brakes properly can mean the difference between cleaning the trail and cleaning your skin. Your front and back brake levers need to be applied differently depending on the situation and the terrain.

DON'T HIT THE SKIDS

Use these tips from mountain bike pros to save your skin.

Ruthie Matthes, 1992 World Cup champion. "In a race, it's important not to use your front brake on descents unless you have to, especially when cornering. If you're going in a straight line, fine, use your front brake to slow for a corner. But then take the turn without brakes or with just a bit of rear braking. Put your outside pedal down so your weight is on the outside of the corner. Keep your weight back, especially if it's a steep descent. This goes hand-in-hand with not using the front brake because when you do, your weight automatically moves forward and you risk going over the handlebar."

Tom Hillard, Specialized coach. "If you skid, you've failed. You need to find the maximum braking point, which is just before the tire starts skidding. It's better to slow gradually than to lock up the brakes. Start by shifting your weight back, rising off the saddle and extending your arms. As you get better, squeeze the front brake harder and the rear brake less, to prevent skidding. Motorcycle riders can brake so well that the rear wheel begins to leave the ground. Shoot for the point at which the rear tire still contacts the ground, but the braking is really happening in front."

Ned Overend, six-time NORBA national champion and pro mountain bike racer and coach. "The front wheel can break loose in a turn if you brake too hard, so look for an area where you can get braking traction beforehand. Pull hard on both brakes when you're in the straightaway. But when you're in the turn, go easy on the front."

Peter Swenson, Specialized pro. "The front brake is important, but lay off it in sand or loose stuff. You see people's forearms rippling trying to pull on the brakes in that kind of terrain. Instead, let the front wheel roll and carry a little more speed for a few seconds until you're through it."

Todd Tanner, Specialized pro. "Try to get comfortable when you're on the verge of locking up the wheels. Sometimes—if you can do it without ruining the trail—practice skidding with the rear wheel and letting go just before you slide out. This helps you get used to the feeling."

TWO BRAKING DRILLS

Drill 1. Place some cones in the middle of a downhill that has a good runout. First apply the back brake only at that spot without skidding. Then apply both to see how much quicker you can stop. Then use just the front, being careful to avoid going over the bar.

Drill 2. Descend a steep hill as slowly as possible. Your tires will be on the verge of control, and any mistake will cause you to fall, but you'll learn braking control. This can be hard. Some riders say the slower you go, the faster things happen.

GOING UP ㊷

By the <u>Mountain Bike</u> and <u>Bicycling</u> Staffs

Few things can be as frustrating for beginning riders as a great ride that turns into a hike-a-bike up every hill. Many riders wrongly believe that they don't have the strength to climb many hills, when in fact they just don't have the skill. Climbing technique is key to making it up not only steep ascents, but short hills and rollers, too. Besides, pushing your bike up takes more energy than riding up.

CLIMBING TIPS FROM THE PROS

Take the following advice from the pros to get over the hump.

Tom Hillard, Specialized coach. "Keep just enough weight on the front wheel to maintain steering ability. As the hill gets steeper, shift your weight forward by moving your upper body closer to the handlebar and sliding forward on the saddle. In rocky conditions you'll need to stand to allow the bike to float underneath you. This also gives you more power to heave up and over larger rocks and ledges and more control over what the back wheel is doing."

Ned Overend, six-time NORBA national champion and pro mountain bike racer and coach. "The worst thing to do on a steep climb is to move your body weight forward as you would on a road bike. This takes your weight off the rear wheel, and you lose traction. Instead, bend at the waist and pull back on the bar, not up.

"Don't mash the pedals. Pedal in circles, so power pulses don't cause the wheel to break loose. You want your legs to be turning over fast enough to keep momentum over obstacles. One way to practice this is with one-legged pedaling. Drive your leg toward the bar, then drag your heel back.

World champion Ruthie Matthes's secret to going up, up and away: She never leaves the saddle.

"As you climb, think of what your neck and upper chest are doing. If these muscles are tense it will be hard to breathe. You don't want to use muscles that aren't required for the climb. I like to do a pronounced exhale once in a while, like Lamaze breathing, to relax."

Ruthie Matthes, 1992 World Cup champion. "On the road, I usually stood on climbs. But this often doesn't work off-road, especially when it's steep, muddy, rocky or loose. It's tempting to get out of the saddle, but you're more likely to crash, go off the best line or have to stop. So I just disciplined myself to do rides where I wouldn't get out of the saddle at all, even if it was a road ride and I knew I could stand and be more comfortable. It sounds like a small thing, but I had to work on it a lot.

"I also move my weight back on climbs to keep the rear wheel in contact with the ground—of course with enough weight on the front to avoid doing a wheelie. It may feel like my weight is evenly distributed, but I know that about 70% of it is over the rear wheel."

John Tomac, 1994 NORBA downhill champion. "To master steep ascents, combine the best aspects of seated and out-of-the-saddle climbing. Rise above the seat to increase leverage and power. To keep the front wheel down and on course, curl your upper body forward almost as you would if seated. Finally, bend your arms to absorb shock and lift the front wheel over rocks."

Wayne Croasdale, Specialized pro. "For short climbs and rollers, use your momentum. Sprint into them, then downshift one click at a time as you come out. Really use those gears and try to pedal the whole thing."

Peter Swenson, Specialized pro. "Keep a stable upper body. Once your head begins to rock, it can cause problems. You can get away with it on the road, but off-road excessive upper-body movement can cause you to lose traction in the loose stuff. Also, you shouldn't have your hands on the bar-ends if the trail is loose. That gives you too much turning torque, and the wheel will slide out."

CLIMBING DRILL

For maximum traction, get to know where your back wheel is. A lot of riders don't know that the back and front tires follow different lines, with the rear going inside the path of the front. Place a rock on smooth ground and make repeated figure eights around it. First, pass the front wheel to the outside of the rock and the rear to the inside, coming as close to it with the rear as possible. Then, pass both wheels around the outside, again coming as close to the rock as possible. Finally, pass the front wheel around the outside of the rock and roll over it with the rear.

Avoiding the Downhill Slide
COMING DOWN ㊸
By the <u>Mountain Bike</u> and <u>Bicycling</u> Staffs

For most riders, riding down is more intimidating than riding up. Since the physical penalty is much greater if you biff on a descent, it's common to overuse your brakes (or use them incorrectly) or develop bad body position on the bike. Although most descents are ridable, you should never attempt to ride down if you don't feel confident. Use the following tips from pro riders, and practice the drill. You'll be going down in no time.

HOW THE PROS COME DOWN

Ruthie Matthes, 1992 World Cup champion. "It's important to stay relaxed. If I find myself tensing up, it's time to back off and return to my level of safety. Listen to yourself because when you push too hard and crash, next time you have a fear barrier to get through. Sometimes, though, it's safer to go a little faster. When you go too slow, the bumps seem bigger, you can't bunny-hop things and you're just riding the brakes, which can cause a skid that could take you out. Look ahead as far as you can. Sometimes you're in the bushes and you can only see five feet in front. But if you can look 50 feet ahead, do it."

Dave Cullinan, 1992 world downhill champion. "Keep your arms, legs and hands flexed and relaxed during high-speed descents. Your body can bust trail shocks as well as any suspension."

Silvia Furst, 1992 cross-country world champion. "Don't use straight arms on descents. People tend to tense and lock their arms when they should be using their arms and legs as suspension. Relax and try to be one with the bike. And if it's steep, move your weight back, behind the seat."

Six-time NORBA national champion Ned Overend keeps his butt low, his back arched and pressure on his pedals when going down.

Peter Swenson, Specialized pro. "Stay in touch with the saddle. Even if you're standing, pinch it with your thighs for control. Sometimes you can steer this way—you don't even need to turn the wheel. It helps you stay in control and know what the bike is doing."

Ned Overend, six-time NORBA national champion and pro mountain bike racer and coach. "Use a way-back position to improve control on high-speed descents. Pressure on the pedals and the strength of your lower back muscles will keep you properly aligned. Keeping your butt low and back slightly arched will improve your control. Eyes up.

"On rock-strewn descents, eye the path of least resistance and your front wheel will follow. Keep your weight back and off the saddle, don't lock the front brake and let the wheel drop like a fresh mountain stream. Resist the temptation to make lots of small steering corrections."

Todd Tanner, Specialized pro. "Get set up early to change your line before you get into trouble. Control your speed as you start. You've lost control if you have to skid in the middle."

Tom Hillard, Specialized coach. "Keep your body in a neutral position, standing slightly off the saddle. This means that if you took your hands off the bar, you wouldn't fall forward or back. And remember that speed is your friend. Most of the time the faster you go, the more stable you are, due to the gyroscopic stability of the wheels.

"Also, falling is okay. What's not good is not knowing why you fell. Don't waste a perfectly good fall, or you'll just have to do it again. Treat it as a physics lesson."

Steve Tilford, Specialized pro. "Don't be afraid to go straight down some rough sections and let your shock fork do the work. Sometimes that's the best way."

DOWNHILL DRILL

Mark a spot where you instinctively start braking for a downhill corner. The next time through, pick a spot that's farther forward. Keep moving this spot up until you find your personal maximum for the corner.

Getting by the Other Guy
MAKING PASSES ⓐ⓪

By Geoff Drake

In an ideal passing situation, the trail either widens slightly or splits for a few feet. But to make the perfect pass, you have to look past the rider in front of you. Find a spot or several corners near the finish and get them dialed perfectly. These are the places where you can make your move.

PRO PASSING TIPS

Use these tips from Specialized riders the next time you need to make your move.

Steve Tilford, Specialized pro. "Sometimes you have to wait until later in a race when people are tired. Then, when you see about two handlebar widths' room, come on strong and tell them which side you're on. Also, the start is so important because if the course narrows to singletrack, you'll be stuck and can lose a lot of time. That's why it's important to train to get your heart rate up high for a short period, then back off to avoid blowing up."

Silvia Furst, 1992 cross-country world champion. "If it's possible, always pass on the inside of a turn because the distance is shorter."

PASSING DRILL

Find a partner and have him ride down singletrack at about 80 percent of maximum speed. Pass him, riding at 90 to 100 percent. Then slow to 80 percent and let your partner pass you. Keep leapfrogging this way.

MORE POINTERS FROM THE PROS ④⑤

By Dan Koeppel

First rule of running a mountain bike camp: Make sure the showers work. And work well.

There were, to be fair, *some* showers that functioned beautifully at Oracle, Arizona's Triangle Y Ranch, where Team Cannondale members convened to tutor, nurture and dispense the two-wheeled equivalent of free love to 150 tip-starved campers from around the world. The showers in the team quarters worked fine, for example. Ditto the secret shower that a few campers found behind the makeshift bike shop.

Not so the primary cleanliness facilities. These showers worked only when you held in the push-button faucets—a prank-proof reminder that this place functions as a kiddie camp in the summer. To make things worse, some campers were a full mile from the shower room.

Then again, when you're spending five fun-filled days at the off-road gulag, who cares if you stay dirty? The riding was spectacular: miles of desert fire road, singletrack, climbs racing more than 5,000 feet and the screaming downhills that followed. The food was pretty fair.

Perhaps best of all was the company. Campers got to shred with downhill world champ Missy Giove, cling with World Champion Alison Sydor, trade deep philosophical insights with downhill stud Myles Rockwell and sample Camembert cheese with ace downhill skinhead Franck Roman.

The photographer and I trailed these superstars, notebook open and camera clicking. Here are the pros' tips, random hints, secrets and strategies. Let the tipfest begin!

ALISON SYDOR

A high-key, super-powerful rider, Alison Sydor is the reigning cross-country women's world champ. Her tips are especially useful for riders who want to make the transition from fun-in-the-dirt riding to competition—or for riders who want to use skills honed by competition on their weekend jaunts.

No secrets. "There's no secret to getting better. You just have to ride your bike and ride with riders who are better than you."

Little secrets. "Everybody's situation and progress are going to be different. All you can do is assess the level you're at and aim to be a bit better. Patience is the most important component of improvement."

Be prepared. "Focusing on results can be intimidating. What I try to concentrate on are the things I can control—my fitness, my psychology, the technology. If you control those things, the results will take care of themselves."

Blind obedience. "Don't always try to break the techniques you're trying to learn down into their individual steps. You might do better by blindly following a rider who does the thing you want to learn very well. You'll lose your inhibitions and find yourself doing things you never thought you could do."

For women only. "The most important thing for women who want to compete is to not see it as a hobby. You have to be interested in performance—in seeing how far you can push yourself."

Tech chic. "One of the biggest things a woman can do to improve her performance is check her brake levers. Almost every lever I've used has been hard for my hands to reach. I couldn't believe how much my downhill performance improved when I switched to levers that I could actually reach." Sydor's lever of choice: Dia-Compe's politically correct PC-7.

Over and over. "The more you pre-ride a course, the shorter and shorter the loops get, the shorter and shorter the climbs get. I try to pre-ride enough so that I can do the entire race on autopilot. The idea is to get to the point where all your energy is used moving the bike forward—not figuring out how you'll do it."

TINKER JUAREZ

NORBA National Champion and splendid hairstyle expert Tinker Juarez rides big—and quietly. He's known for a steady, hard-pounding style and for paying his cross-country dues for years before finally winning the 1994 National Championship series.

Tinker Juarez, winner of the 1994 National Championship series, began by riding up small hills as fast as he could, then tackling bigger hills at the same speed.

Not hitting the road. "I don't train that much on the road—once or twice a week at the most. I just have more fun riding in the dirt. If I do ride the road, I try to keep the ride under 30 miles—though I do go hard." Sure, this flies against conventional wisdom and alternate tippage. But who cares? It's your life.

Going up. "I started by trying to ride up small hills as fast as I possibly could. Then I went to bigger hills, trying to maintain that speed. I didn't do it all at once. Not too many riders pull away on the climbs. If that's an ability you think you can develop, it's well worth it."

On the other hand ... "More and more courses are getting more and more technically difficult, especially on the downhill sections. If you're a good descender and can shave time on the descents, you'll do well."

Add climbing. "It's not initially that anybody says `I love to climb.' It's hard. But once you get good at it, it will become fun. It will become natural. Then you'll start to enjoy it." Maybe.

MISSY GIOVE

To boil 1994 World Downhill Champion Missy Giove's world view into a few pert, pithy tips is to do a disservice to off-roading's reigning high-speed poseable action figure. But what the heck. Let's give it a shot.

Body positioning. Giove is well-known for working her bike with her body. Here are a few preferred stances.

- Upper body/arms: "Keep them open and wide to help you breathe."
- Climbs: "Before you enter a hard-work section, relax your shoulders so you're really loose."
- Rough stuff: "Throw your weight forward and over rocks and obstacles."

Stops and starts. Trying to restart on a steep uphill section? "Hold your brakes in," says Giove. "Then start pedaling."

Hits and misses. When faced with hitting a wall or a pickup truck, says Giove, "Choose the wall." This happened on a winter training ride in Durango. "It was my fault," Giove recalls. "So after I scraped myself off the wall, I apologized to the truck driver."

MYLES ROCKWELL AND FRANCK ROMAN

Rockwell, who placed third in the 1995 NORBA National Championship Downhill Series, is a strong descender well-suited for fast,

Volvo/Cannondale rider Franck Roman demonstrates how to do a wheelie.

scary U.S. courses. The Euro counterpart to Rockwell is Franck Roman, also on the Cannondale squad. Roman's daring, technical style is perfect for the continent's rocky, twisty, damp downhills.

Rockwell and Roman want to see you get down the mountain as fast as you can, in one piece and with a whole mess of style. Here are their best low-down dirty hints.

Pump it. "I try to use every twist, every up and down, to maintain speed—and accelerate," says Rockwell. "I call this pumping the terrain." Use your own terrain at home. Try to push the bike into the ground, try to fly off bumps—play with your local dirt—and see what makes you faster.

Winter training. "I ride my bike to feel good in the winter," says Rockwell. "I try to make it playtime as much as possible, to feel comfortable. I also mix it up—I like to try other balance sports, like skateboarding."

Roman in winter. "During the winter I ride road bikes and lift weights; downhilling is about leg speed and power. Spinning and leg exercises help both."

Do it in the dark. "On European descents," says Roman, "there are lots of trees and rocks. Knowing how to get around them helps me on every course. I try to know about dirt and ground. You can find a little piece of forest that's dark and rocky to practice in. Learn how to read the terrain. If you're approaching an area that's in shadow, you know it might be muddy. If there's light, it might be dry."

Know your legs. "Measure your fitness as a downhiller by being aware of how you feel on the uphill portions of the course," says

Myles Rockwell on the essence of downhilling: "The whole purpose is fun. Devote yourself and have a genuine passion. If you bang your head against the wall and scream, `I want to get good now,' it isn't going to happen."

Rockwell. "Downhill fitness is all about acceleration, and you need to train for those moments."

Screwup advice. "Brush off the dirt, pick the weeds out of your hair and relax. Walk back up the course and see where your tracks went. Analyze what you've done. Ask somebody who saw you wipe out what you did wrong. If you don't have a broken bike or body, try it again."

Rockwell Airborne Express. "You learn to jump by inspecting the jump, knowing where you'll get airborne and knowing where you'll land."

Your first downhill race. "Know your course," says Roman. "I ride a course for six hours a day, every day, for a week before a race. The secret to going fast is having the technique and knowing the terrain."

Part 6 Ready for

Racing

YOUR FIRST RACE ㊻

By Dan Koeppel

On a training ride with a friend, I was engaging in some wishful thinking about the upcoming NORBA season. "My problem last year was that I was unrealistic," I said. "This year, I'm going to be more reasonable. I want to place above the middle of the pack in the Kamikaze. And I want one—just one—top-ten finish in a NORBA."

I was sounding pretty tough for a thirtysomething sport-class bum, which is what I am. I'd just finished a full season of racing with astonishingly average results. Bottom third at Cactus Cup. DNF (did not finish) at Big Bear. A couple of top-half finishes in the California Points Series. Very middling performance at the huge NORBA race at Mammoth, where I had hoped my season would peak.

My friend took a deep breath. "I used to think I could do well in the cross-country races," he said. "I had goals like you. But then I realized it isn't possible. There are just too many guys who are just too good."

As we headed down the hill, I knew he was right. I'm a good rider, but I'll never be much more than average as a racer. I'm not born for it. I thought back to my first race, years ago, at Connecticut's Williams Lake. It hurt. Four laps of mud and pain. I hated it. No, I loved it. No, wait, I remember now, I hated it. The only reason I wasn't dead last is because a lot of people dropped out. At least I wasn't one of them—but I was slow. Real slow. By the time I finished, they were mapping the course for next season.

But listen to this, because this is the point: That race made me one happy cat.

And that's why you should race. Maybe just once this season or just once in your life. Maybe not at the front, maybe way off the

SETTING YOUR GOAL

How many times do you want to race this year? What do you want to gain from the experience? Your answers will define your experience. Here are three approaches to consider for your first season.

Be ambitious. Race twice a month, April through September. This is going to be tough, and it will require dedication, training and often lots of travel. The benefit is guaranteed vast improvement in your skills, even if you're not trying to win. If you follow this plan, you owe it to yourself to try at least one NORBA national.

Be realistic. Race once a month. Do this and you will still improve without biweekly suffering. If you're lucky enough to have a local points series, you'll gain the advantage of racing against the same people, which lets you measure your own improvement and exact revenge on the others.

Just have fun. Race once or twice. Maybe plan a vacation around one event. Even at this low level of participation, you'll have a blast. Ride as fast as you can, be as aggressive as you want to be and don't sweat the details.

back. Whatever. Wherever. Because competition is painful and wonderful and insane and ugly and beautiful, beautiful, beautiful. The fastest, best way to become a better mountain biker is to race. The fastest, best way to get in touch with the pure physical exhilaration and hardship of this sport is to race. The fastest way to go faster is to race. And there's only one good way to learn how. Race.

That's why I'm going to keep doing it. This love-hate thing gets my dander up. I like that. And despite what my riding buddy says, I'm going to keep those goals. Sure, they may be impossible dreams, but daring the impossible is part of what attracted me to mountain biking in the first place.

Just the fact that I can show up for the sport-class race in Mammoth or Big Bear or some other mecca and ride my bike on the same world-class course that challenges John Tomac, Ned Overend and Juli Furtado—that seems pretty impossible in itself. What if a baseball fan were allowed to play on a major league diamond or if a football fan could do battle in the Rose Bowl? They'd jump at the chance.

The racing side of our sport is still so new. Even on the pro/elite level, there have been only six world championships. On the local

Six-time NORBA national champion Ned Overend burns up the singletrack. His secrets: practice, persistence and control.

level, the number of races increases every year. Right now lots of riders—maybe you—are on the verge of joining the action. Unlike road racing, there's no Euro/leg-shaver snobbiness to turn you off. Mountain bike racing is more laid-back, like a festival, a Lollapallooza of self-challenge.

Chances are you've been thinking about it. You're intrigued. You're thinking maybe this is the year for your first race, and you're wondering how well you'd do. There's only one way to know: Jump at the chance. It's time to take the leap.

HINTS FROM A LIVING LEGEND

No one is more revered on the racing circuit than Ned Overend, six-time NORBA national champion and pro mountain bike racer and coach. Here's his best advice for your first race.

Know thy course. Walking the course before each race is key. Walk it slowly, noting the parts that might give you trouble and the spots where you might gain time.

Practice! If there are tough technical sections, rehearse them several times. That's especially important if your handling skills aren't good yet.

Stay in control. If you don't have a chance to pre-ride, you really need to maintain a controllable speed for whatever's around the next corner. You lose more time by crashing than by being in control.

Expect the unexpected. At smaller races you can find all sorts of stuff on the course—cars, motorcycles, hikers. Be careful. Never assume that a course is closed just because the organizers say it is.

Pick your opponents. In your first races, just compete against yourself and against the course. You want to do as well as you can, but don't pace yourself based on the other riders. Pace yourself based on your experience doing hard rides of that length.

Don't start too fast. If you think you'll be at the front of the pack, by all means go out fast. Otherwise, start at your regular riding pace. One exception: If there's a lot of dust or traffic in the middle of the pack, you might think about an early break.

Beware the downhills. Most serious injuries occur in sport and beginner classes. People get so excited that they tend to ride over their heads. You don't win races on downhills, usually. You win with consistent riding.

Review the results. When it's over, look at how you did. Did you go out too fast and end up slower overall? Did you have problems on the flats? Did you get dropped on climbs? Did you have mechanical problems? If you identify your weaknesses, you can address them. Do the same thing for your strengths. If there were sections in which you put time on your competitors, give yourself a pat on the back—and work to add to those strengths in your second race.

BASIC TRAINING ④⑦

By Oliver Starr

You want to race but you're not sure if you're ready. Sure, you can beat your friends to the top of a climb during your weekly foray on your local trail, but it's another thing to put it on the line in front of hundreds of spectators and other riders.

As a professional racer and coach of some top-ranked NORBA pros, I know the kind of hard work it takes to be successful. I also know the consequence of trying to do too much too soon. To help you become race-ready, I've devised this training program and thrown in lots of hard-earned tips that I've picked up in my 20 years of racing.

THE ULTIMATE TRAINING SCHEDULE

Proven training schedules consist of three components: long, lower-intensity rides to build endurance, high-intensity sessions to build speed and rest days to give your body time to recover. Finding the right combination of these components is the key to a successful training program.

Building Endurance

Because the ability to hang tough and make it to the finish line is the hallmark of every successful racer, you need endurance rides in any program. In a race, it doesn't matter who gets up the first climb fastest, but rather who crosses the finish line first. You have to be able to push hard for an extended period. This means you need to spend a good deal of time just pedaling your bicycle.

The good news is that this type of training is generally the most fun. You don't have to ride hard to get excellent benefits, and in fact, if it hurts or if you find yourself breathing hard, your pace is too high. Endurance rides should be two to three hours (depending on your fitness level; see specific programs) at 55 to 65 percent of your maximum heart rate. (To determine your maximum heart rate, see below.) These rides are an excellent time to explore new trails or accumulate mega-miles on a road bike.

Endurance training is designed to help you become more efficient by teaching your body to use stored fats to power your muscles. Even the leanest athlete has enough calories stored as fat to run more than 100 miles, so for the purposes of racing a mountain bike, fat stores are almost inexhaustible. But only through long-distance training can you teach your body to access this fuel, sparing more efficient carbohydrate stores for higher-intensity efforts.

Building Speed:
Intervals and Sprints

While low-key endurance workouts make up the bulk of your training, they don't provide complete fitness. You also need to include bouts of high-intensity work, called intervals. Intervals are designed to improve your aerobic capacity so you can ride harder, longer. A successive group of intervals is known as a set.

For mountain bikers, intervals can provide a fantastic descent into the realm that some refer to as "shaking hands with God." These painful sessions should be highly structured, which may seem contrary to the ideals associated with mountain biking, but the long-term benefits are well worth the effort and completely necessary for a big payoff on race day.

There are hundreds of types of interval workouts, but the basics remain the same—periods of intense effort followed by periods of recovery. Intervals can be done on the road or on your mountain bike, but choose an area that allows you to go consistently hard (85 to 90 percent of max) for the duration of each effort. Or you can use a stationary trainer. Because the efforts are so intense, being away from traffic is a good idea. Plus, think of the intervals you could do while watching a video of the Kamikaze or blaring your favorite rock group from the stereo.

As your legs will quickly tell you, the harder you push yourself, the shorter the duration will become. In general, two to five minutes at 85 to 90 percent with one to three minutes "off" is a good basic interval workout. "Off" means backing way off—your heart rate should drop to 120 bpm. You know you're cooked when you can't maintain a cadence of 80 to 90 percent or can't reach your target heart rate.

If you're having trouble getting your heart rate to drop between efforts, you may be pushing too hard or your fitness level may need some improvement. Intervals should be done no more than twice per week—once if you're racing, and no closer than 72 hours before a race.

Nothing can be more frustrating than riding a great race, getting to the finish in contention for the win and being out-sprinted by some ex-roadie who managed to hang on to your wheel for that last singletrack descent. In order to avoid the ignominy of this situation, you need to add sprints—a variation of intervals—to your weekly training schedule.

Sprints are simple enough and can even be added in to your endurance rides. Here's how to do them. Pick a spot about 150 to 200 yards up the trail and go as hard as you possibly can until you get to that spot. You should nearly blow chunks if you've done it correctly. Three to five sprints about 15 to 25 minutes apart should shred your legs. If not, you need to go harder. Sprinting uphill increases power, downhill improves speed and flat sprints help with both.

Rest

It doesn't matter how fit you are if you're fatigued at the start line. That's why rest is important not only before races, but also as a regular part of your training routine. A rest phase lets your body adapt to the demands that training places upon it, heal any minor injuries sustained during your hard workout and replenish depleted fuel stores.

Usually, the day before a race and the day following a race are reserved for rest. If you're the kind of person who can't stand to spend the day on the couch, don't. If you must get out, take an extremely slow, easy ride (55 percent of max). Taking a walk or going for a swim can also be therapeutic on your rest days.

THREE TOP TRAINING PROGRAMS

Below are training programs for riders of various fitness levels, available training time and goals. Each program is devised to get you fit during the race season and keep you fit when it's over. During the season, substitute a real race for one or both of your high-intensity days. Each program is designed to provide you with basic workouts that are applicable to entry-level competition.

As you progress, you'll be better able to determine what you need to focus on to maximize your competitive success. Also, remember that these are merely guidelines—feel free to experiment

until you find the specific mix of rest and harder workouts █████
you the best results.

A few caveats: Before you undertake any strenuous new r█
get yourself checked out by a physician, especially if you ha█
blood pressure or heart disease or if you have a family hist█
these diseases. Also, remember that stress on the job or at home ███
detract from your workout. Mind, body and soul must be working
together to enable you to reach your potential.

WHICH PLAN IS FOR YOU?

To determine which program is right for you, check out the following descriptions and use the program that sounds most like you.

Program 1. You ride three or four times a week and have never competed. Your rides are usually less than two hours, but may be at least three hours on weekends. The intensity of your rides is generally moderate to low.

Program 2. You typically ride four or five days a week, with at least two rides that are more than two hours. At least one time per week you do an intense workout either alone or with friends. Some of your rides exceed three hours. You may have competed in road cycling or in some other endurance sport.

Program 3. You have previous competitive experience in another endurance sport—road cycling, running or triathlon. Generally, you have the time and the inclination to train daily and are able to regularly ride for two or more hours. You usually do one to three harder rides a week and tend to be stronger than your companions on group outings.

Program 1

Monday: Generally, a rest and recovery day. If you choose to ride, limit yourself to less than an hour of very easy spinning (55 to 65 percent of max). A walk or a light swim is also okay. Total time: less than one hour.

Tuesday: Sprints. Warm up (55 to 65 percent of max) for about 30 minutes before beginning your first sprint. Ride 12 to 15 seconds at maximum effort. Recover for 10 minutes, then repeat twice more. Cool down for 15 minutes following your last sprint. Total time: 1 hour, 5 minutes.

Wednesday: Endurance day. Ride 2½ to 3 hours at an easy to moderate pace (65 to 75 percent of max). Total time: 2½ to 3 hours.

Thursday: Intervals. Warm up (55 to 65 percent of max) for 30

..ninutes, then ride 2 minutes at 85 to 90 percent of max, followed by 2 minutes at 60 percent. Repeat twice more, then cool down for 15 minutes. Total time: 1 hour.

Friday: Recovery day. See Monday.

Saturday: Intense group ride or race. The ride should be no more than 2 hours at a hard pace (85 percent of max). If you're racing on Sunday, do a short ride with two 30-second efforts of very high intensity (90 percent of max). Total time: 1 to 2 hours.

Sunday: Low-intensity (55 to 65 percent of max) ride of no more than 2 hours. If you raced the previous day, take it extremely easy. Total time: 1 to 2 hours.

Weekly total: Minimum of 6 hours 35 minutes; maximum of 11 hours 35 minutes.

Program 2

Monday: See Monday, Program 1.

Tuesday: Sprints. Warm up (55 to 65 percent of max) for about 30 minutes before beginning your first sprint. Ride 12 to 15 seconds at maximum effort. Recover for 7 minutes, then repeat four more times. Cool down for 15 minutes following your last sprint. Total time: 1 hour, 15 minutes.

Wednesday: See Wednesday, Program 1.

Thursday: Intervals. Warm up (55 to 65 percent of max) for 30 minutes. Then ride 2 minutes at 85 to 90 percent of max, followed by 2 minutes at 60 percent. Cool down for 15 minutes, then repeat twice more, with a 15-minute cool down between sets. Total time: 1 hour 30 minutes.

Friday: Recovery day. See Monday, Program 1.

Saturday: See Saturday, Program 1.

Sunday: See Sunday, Program 1.

Weekly total: Minimum of 7 hours, 15 minutes; maximum of 11 hours, 45 minutes.

Program 3

Monday: See Monday, Program 1.

Tuesday: Sprints. Warm up (55 to 65 percent of max) for about 30 minutes. Then ride 15 to 20 seconds at maximum effort. Recover for 7 minutes, then repeat six more times. Cool down for 15 minutes following your last sprint. Total time: 1 hour 30 minutes.

Wednesday: Endurance day. Ride 3 to 4 hours at an easy to moderate pace (65 to 75 percent of max). Total time: 3 to 4 hours.

Thursday: Intervals. Warm up (55 to 65 percent of max) for 30 minutes. Then ride 2 minutes at 85 to 90 percent of max, followed by 2 minutes at 60 percent. Cool down for 15 minutes, then repeat four more times, with a 15-minute cool down between sets. Ride 5 minutes at 85 to 90 percent of max, followed by 3 minutes at 60 percent. Cool down for 15 minutes, then repeat once, followed by a 15-minute cool down. Total time: 2 hours, 50 minutes.

Friday: Recovery day. See Monday, Program 1.

Saturday: See Saturday, Program 1.

Sunday: Low-intensity (55 to 65 percent of max) ride of no more than 2 or 3 hours. If you raced the previous day, take it extremely easy. Total time: 1½ to 3 hours.

Weekly total: Minimum of 10 hours; maximum of 15 hours, 20 minutes.

USING A HEART RATE MONITOR

One key to every training schedule is knowing how hard your heart is pumping blood during a workout. But taking your pulse is nearly impossible (and dangerous) while riding. What's more, when pulse rates are elevated, it can be difficult to count correctly. To get an accurate measure of your performance and to effectively track your training, consider using a heart rate monitor.

Heart rate monitors have become an essential training tool for

A heart rate monitor is a must-have for many serious mountain bikers. Juli Furtado, 1995 World Cup champ, has relied heavily on this training tool.

most serious mountain bikers. The best ones are wireless models, in which you wear a chest belt that transmits to a wristwatch-like receiver on the handlebar. Monitors are comfortable, durable and relatively easy to use. Basic units display heart rate only, which is enough for many cyclists. Fancier models feature high and low alarms so that you can set a target zone, record your workout and even download info into a computer.

Here are ten tips for using a heart rate monitor.

1. Read the instructions. Then read them again. Become familiar with the features and operation of your monitor so that you can use it to maximum advantage. This tip is basic, but it's key.

2. Determine your maximum heart rate. The key to training with a monitor is knowing your ticker's top end. Various formulas will get you in the ballpark—for example, 220 minus your age, or 210 minus your age, multiplied by 0.65. Or use an indoor trainer and increase gear size every three minutes while keeping a 90 cadence. Start in an easy ratio and don't stop until you absolutely can't maintain the rpm. But to be precise, you might undergo a medically supervised test.

3. Drench the electrodes. In our experience, nothing is more important for reliable performance than wetting the electrode strips on the chest belt as well as the skin that's under them. Use water, saliva, a saline solution or EKG gel sold in medical supply stores. Most transmitters will work if they're worn over an undershirt, as long as the fabric is wet.

4. Dry the electrodes. After riding, dry the electrodes to deactivate the transmitter and prolong battery life. For the same reason, never store a transmitter in an unbreathable container—such as a plastic bag—where moisture can collect. If the transmitter snaps off the belt, remove it between uses to save the battery.

5. Tighten the chest strap. While straps vary somewhat in width and style of quick-release buckle, our male and female testers found all brands equally comfortable, and all are elastic, washable and adjustable. We found it best to make the straps quite snug to ensure good electrode contact and to accommodate slight stretching as they become damp with sweat. We could always tell that we were wearing a strap, but they didn't feel uncomfortable or restrictive during deep breathing.

6. Beware of erratic readings. Ultra high or low readings can occur in any monitor if you're too close to another cyclist who is wearing one or if you get near strong electromagnetic sources such as high-voltage power lines. Normal function should resume as soon as you're out of range.

7. Avoid extreme heat or cold. Most monitors will operate in a temperature range from the mid-teens to about 120°F. Chest belt transmitters can beam their signal through several layers of clothing, but subfreezing temperatures can slow monitor response and reduce battery life.

8. Heed warnings about water resistance. Some monitors can be harmed by rain or heavy sweat, while others can be used for swimming. But even with these, you risk a damaging leak should you depress a monitor button when submerged.

9. Forget fancy bike brackets. Instead, put a 1½-inch-wide piece of light, cheap pipe insulation around the handlebar to mount a wristwatch-style monitor. This dense foam helps dampen shock, and it compresses slightly to let you securely tighten the strap.

10. Don't expect perfect performance. Durability may be less than you'd hope for in a fairly expensive product. With regular use, belts, batteries and even transmitters will need to be replaced, and the monitor could require service. Most monitors have a one-year warranty.

SURVIVAL
OF THE FITTEST ㊽

By Geoff Drake

The rarefied air and unending singletrack of Durango, Colorado, has produced some of America's best mountain bikers—including Daryl Price. Though sometimes overshadowed by his neighbors John Tomac and Ned Overend, Price has earned a reputation for consistency at the highest level of competition. He has placed in the top ten three times in world championships. Price also had a stellar junior career, earning national cyclocross titles in 1986 and 1987 and a national road championship in 1987. He devoted himself to the burgeoning sport of mountain biking in 1988. He was on the Specialized team from 1989 to 1992 and was a protégé of six-time NORBA national champion Ned Overend.

Here's Price's advice on preparing for your first off-road race.

BASIC TRAINING

If you want to win a race, you need to focus on perfecting the basic but crucial skills that every great rider must develop. Here's Price's advice.

On mixing road and mountain biking: "It's important to become familiar with your mountain bike, particularly if you're coming from the road. If you ride the road bike all the time, you'll never be at ease in a mountain bike race, and you'll never do your best. So ride off-road a minimum of three times per week if you have little experience racing mountain bikes. If you go back and forth easily, you can ride the road more.

"I use the road bike more to do recovery-type rides, high-repetition spinning and sprinting. It's good to have your legs experience the rapid turnover and reduced rolling resistance. In comparison to riding your mountain bike, road bikes give the feeling that the wind is always at your back."

On learning off-road technique: "The most important thing is to ride behind someone who's good and see where the clean line is, and even where they blow it. As you watch, you become more comfortable doing what they're doing. It's also valuable to do laps of the same short course. The repetition teaches you the fastest way to take each section.

"It's hard to say what improves your downhill ability. It seems like it isn't technique or skill; it's just lunacy. If you try to go too fast in training, you'll get in over your head and crash. That's when the trail gets trashed, too. You want to be in control. That's the only way you'll enjoy it."

On setting a training program: "Every week I do at least one long (four- to five-hour), slow ride at a heart rate of less than about 140 beats per minute. Because it's low-intensity, I can even do it after a hard day. Usually it's on the road bike. You really can't do it on a mountain bike because the rolling resistance means you can't recover. This ride also burns fat because it's at a low heart rate. I really try to keep it below 130, but late in the ride that's tough. I go on nice country roads and enjoy myself.

"Then I do one interval ride on- or off-road, usually on Tuesday or Wednesday because that's when I feel fresh after a weekend race. Because there are no flat mountain bike races, I always do intervals on hills. Also, it's hard to motivate myself to do these efforts on the flats.

"It's not as hard mentally to get your heart rate up in the hills. Usually, I'll do a 5-plus-5 interval, which means 5 minutes at anaerobic threshold (the level of effort at which your muscles create lactic acid faster than they can eliminate it), then 5 minutes at a lesser intensity. I do 30 minutes of that, then recover for 30, then do another 30-minute set. If I feel bad I'll do 3-plus-3 instead.

"Or I'll do an extended heart rate effort—for me, that means 30 minutes at 170 or 180. It depends on what I think I need for the upcoming race."

GETTING READY TO RACE

Most of Price's pre-race strategy involves being prepared for the unexpected. Here are his tips.

On preparing to race: "Keep in mind that nothing you do in the days just before the race will help you go faster in that race. It can only hurt you. In general, I start my preparation schedule three days out. On that day I just do one hour easy. The next day I ride the course and make a few spinning efforts up the climbs. That's at a real easy pace, for one or two hours, to get my legs moving and check out the course. The day before I do 90 minutes on the course at a couple of notches below race speed. It needs to be a good tempo so I know how to set up for the corners and what the right line is. You need to learn the course."

On checking your equipment: "Check your equipment the day before, particularly tire pressure. If the course is rocky, you need to run enough to prevent pinch flats. Also, a clean bike is a happy bike, so I try to wash it right after I ride that day. I'll spray the bike, run a rag over it and lubricate it. That means pulling the cables out of their stops and using a light oil on them and oiling the chain. In general, try not to make too many adjustments—just tire and fork pressure. Don't do any equipment changes or derailleur adjustments. Those things will just create stress. Your bike should be dialed by then."

On handling breakdowns: "For the race I carry two CO_2 cartridges, a tube and a multi-tool that includes a chain tool and 4, 5 and 6mm Allen wrenches. I keep it all in a seat pack. I always carry this kit because I get paid to finish. I need as many series points as I can get, and if I don't have tools to fix my bike, it could cost me a national title. My sponsors pay a lot to get me to races, and I don't quit many of them."

On warming up: "I prefer to race in the morning because I can get nervous. Food doesn't settle, and you expend a lot of energy thinking about the race. Sometimes you need to go to the bathroom ten times, even though you know you're not hydrated. In general, you have to try to relax. Don't tinker with your bike. Just lie there, stretch, watch some TV and take in the calories.

"Once you get to the course, do a one-hour warm-up. Start with 30 minutes at a leisurely pace, then do high-intensity 1- to 5-minute efforts. You want to be on the line sweating, with your heart rate high."

RACING TIPS

It's crucial to pace yourself, says Price. But what you do before and after a race is just as important.

On starting a race: "People coming from a road background find the start of mountain bike races to be ballistic. You sit at the start for 15 minutes, then your heart rate goes from 80 to 180 instantly. Everyone's legs feel like cement. It's super-high intensity, and then you just go until you fade. That's basically what a mountain bike race is. So instead of experiencing the start for the first time in a race, ensure that you can go at a high intensity by doing it in training.

"The effort you put in at the start also depends on what the course is like. Some narrow to singletrack quickly, and the position you have going into it is the position you'll have coming out. If you're in 30th going in, you'll be at least a minute behind, and it will be hard to do well. When the course narrows to singletrack, people lose their marbles. People who were your friends are suddenly fighting you for 25th place.

"If there's more doubletrack on the course, you can pace yourself into the start. That means riding the wheels in front of you, but not fighting for them as much."

On pacing yourself: "Treat the race like a time trial. Just go your max. You can pace yourself and catch people who are dying later on, but it's better to go hard from the start. You can also make a special effort on certain sections. For instance, if I'm behind Dave Wiens on a sketchy downhill, I'll try to get by beforehand. And I'll pass Bob Roll before a singletrack section. But I'll follow John Tomac anywhere. Ned Overend, too. They're good on anything. But certain people I'll race into a part of the course.

"I also wear a heart rate monitor, but mostly just to recall the information on a computer afterward. I'll look at it sometimes in a race. I'll never slow if it tells me my heart rate is high (around 190). On the other hand, if I see it's 170, I know I can do 15 bpm more, so I might go harder."

On refueling while racing: "I usually drink one bottle of Energy Surge and have one bottle handed to me during the race. And I have water in a second bottle. I don't use solid food—it's impossible in a mountain bike race. You can hardly drink, much less eat. It's hard to take your hands off the bar."

On cooling down: "It's a good idea to warm down with some easy pedaling after the race, but usually it's unrealistic. You're so tired. First, get clean and get a bottle. Then reward yourself. If you want a Coke, have a Coke. That night, if you want a beer, have one. That's what it's all about. Reward yourself. Get two scoops of ice cream. You have to enjoy the event to the same degree that you sacrificed for it."

EQUIPPED
FOR EXCELLENCE ㊾

By Dan Koeppel

You've decided to race, and you've gotten in shape. Now it's time to make sure that your bike is in peak condition. Here are pro team mechanics' and racers' top equipment tips for beginners.

1. Half-filled tubes. In a race, all repairs are up to you, so you have to be fast. Fill a pair of tubes halfway and stuff them in your jersey pocket. If you flat, you'll save about a minute with this trick.

2. CamelBak/energy drink. Hydration systems from CamelBak and Aquastream allow you to carry a lot of water and let you get to it fast. Hot tip: Put plain water on your back for copious hydration and carry a bottle of energy bev on your bike to make sure you don't bonk.

3. A real outfit. If you have the nerve to carry off baggies and flannel, go for it. But a jersey can be a useful place for a mini-tool or spare tube. And we all know the benefits of Lycra and chamois. If you're in a local club, wear that jersey. You'll really feel honch.

4. Quickfills. Forget the pump. In a race, you want to get in and out of a flat fast. So use instant-fill CO_2 cartridges. If you've never used one, practice first. Bring a spare in case you screw up.

5. Clear-lens glasses. Most courses move in and out of shadow. At high speeds, you need to pick a line fast. Clear lenses help. Iridium-coated lenses don't. Use shaded lenses only on extra-bright courses.

6. Thin grips. Fat, foamy grips don't give you enough response for real racing. They can lead to forearm pain and can get slippery when wet or sweaty. Go with thin rubber models—Onza, Ritchey and ATI are some good brands.

7. Front suspension. A shock lets you go faster over extremely tough terrain. Look for one that's adjustable and fairly light, such as a Rock Shox Quadra or Tange Struts. If you don't have one, don't be intimidated by all the shocks you'll see at the start line. Think of those riders as wimps who need a cushion or use whatever reasoning you need to not get psyched out. And remember this: Three-time world cross-country champion Henrik Djernis still uses a rigid fork.

8. Good tires. If you have a new bike and it cost less than $700, there's a good chance that it has "original equipment" tires that are heavier and less supple than high-quality racing tires. Race tires—such as Specialized Pro Controls, Yeti Pro FROs or Onza Racing Porcs—can be expensive, but they're worth it. Run them at slightly higher pressures than normal to avoid flats.

9. A new chain. Broken chains are one of the least expected—and most common—ways to lose a race. Put a new chain on the week before an important event. Ride it a few times. The reward? Smooth shifts and no worries.

10. Pedals you like. Clips and straps aren't popular on the circuit. But you don't have to go clipless. Don't fall for the hype if you're not comfortable with it. And if you do switch, make sure you have time to practice with the clipless system before the race. Choose Shimano SPD, Onza, Speedplay or other popular systems. Many BMX-bred downhillers, including world champion Mike King, use platform pedals and plain sneakers.

Follow the dots to the ultimate in equipment.

DIRT-IONARY
Making Sense of
Mountain Bike Mumbo Jumbo

By Beth Strickland

Before I became a mountain biker, I thought holes were holes, logs were logs and trees were trees. But on the trail, things are named by how they affect the terrain, not by what they are. Part of becoming a full-fledged mountain biker is learning the lingo. And understanding what each term means can also make you a better rider. Here is some of the most-common trailspeak.

Beginner: The class for first-time racers. You can't stay in beginner for more than one season. Don't expect all beginners to be novice riders, though many are. Beginner courses are usually one lap only—generally 4 to 6 miles.

Biff: To crash.

BMX: Bicycle motocross. This is a smaller version of the mountain bike, with 20-inch wheels and a single speed.

Bonk: To run out of energy. Usually means that a rider isn't eating or drinking enough.

Box vans: Large team trucks, covered with team logos, that follow their sponsored racers to events, transporting bikes and equipment.

Bunny-hop: A way to jump over obstacles such as rocks or logs in which both wheels leave the ground.

Catch air: To ride with both wheels off the ground when your bike hits a natural rise or dip in the trail.

Chainsuck: When the chain doubles back on itself in the middle of a gear shift and gets jammed either between the chainrings or between the crank and the frame.

Cross-country: The standard and most popular type of racing for most off-road events. A cross-country race goes over the hills and through the woods and can—depending on how mean the course designer is—include segments of running, jumping, crashing, descending and climbing. Most courses mix fire road (where you can pass or be passed) with singletrack, where passing is tougher.

Doubletrack: A path wide enough for two cyclists to ride side by side.

Downhill: High-octane, high-powered racing. Most big National Off-Road Bicycle Association (NORBA) events at ski areas include a downhill segment that you can enter. For these, lots of riders wear tougher body armor than for cross-country races. Pros generally ride downhill with dual-suspension.

Dual slalom: Just like skiing, you maneuver between gates on a short downhill course. Unlike downhilling, in which your adversary is the clock, the slalom is a head-to-head tournament. You keep advancing until you lose—or finally win. Preferred by BMX riders. Only at ski-area races.

Endo: To crash by going over the bike's handlebar. Short for end-over-end.

Elite: Top-of-the-line racers.

Expert: This class includes riders with high levels of fitness, aggressiveness and dedication. Many younger pups in the expert class entertain dreams of moving to the pro/elite class—and some do. Expert courses are sometimes the same length as sport courses, sometimes the same as pro courses and sometimes in-between.

Fire road: Roads in the hills just wide enough to allow emergency vehicle access.

Granny gear: Small, lowest gear chainring, used mainly for climbing.

Grundig: The large European electronics company that sponsors the international World Cup circuit in conjunction with the Union Cyclists International. In each of these races, points are awarded to top finishers. The final point total determines the Grundig/World Cup championship.

Gully: This falls away from the side of the trail. Trying to panic-steer out of one can twist you up.

Hill climb: A rapidly declining species of mountain bike racing. While some hill climbs exist (notably Mammoth's Ezakimak—that's Kamikaze backwards), they're being shunned in favor of more popular downhill and slalom events.

Huffy toss: An irreverent event often held at mountain bike festivals. Top prize goes to whoever throws a bike the farthest, although bonus points are sometimes awarded for any components that fly off.

IMBA: International Mountain Bicycling Association.

NORBA: National Off-Road Bicycle Association.

NORBA National: While NORBA sanctions hundred of events, only a handful are part of its national championship series. In each of these races, points are awarded to top finishers. The final point total determines the NORBA national championship.

Off-camber turns: These slope down on the outside of the curve, making inertia and other things conspire to throw you off the trail and down the hill.

Privateer: An unsponsored racer.

Pro: You know this story. Besides the 20 or 30 major name-brand pro racers, several dozen others, including unsponsored racers known as elites or privateers, compete on this circuit.

Rankings: NORBA has developed a computer-based system that, for the first time, provides regional rankings for riders all the way down to the sport category.

Retrogrouch: Someone who is slow to accept the latest clothing and technical upgrades, preferring instead to use equipment from the last decade. He operates according to the maxim "If it ain't broke, why replace it?" Opposite of technogeek.

Rut: Another erosion product. It's narrower—usually about a diabolical tire-grabbing width—and travels more or less along a trail.

Sag wagon: The vehicle that follows a supported tour to carry the cyclists' belongings as well as the cyclists, should they get too tired to ride.

Sandbagger: A weasel-like species who stays in an easier race category when he really should move up. NORBA rules mandate a class upgrade after a certain number of top finishes, but it's hard to enforce.

Scot-trials: A variation of trials, these involve trail racing between sections that are marked off to be ridden as trials. Time is added for dabs on the trials sections. The winner is determined by time, not points.

Singletrack: A path so narrow that two cyclists can't ride side by side.

Sport: Ah, the teeming masses! There are more riders in sport class than in all other categories combined. You have folks just edging out of the beginner class and riders who really should be competing in expert category—but like winning in sport too much to leave (see "Sandbagger"). Sport courses usually run two or three laps.

Swag: Prizes. Free stuff.

Switchback: A 90-degree or greater turn on a road or trail. Trail builders blaze these turns when the slope is to steep to go straight up or down.

Technogeek: Someone who sports all the latest technical gizmos on his bike (whether he knows how to use them or not). Opposite of retrogrouch.

Tech support: You'll find box vans full of mechanics at bigger NORBA events. Local bike shops set up at smaller events. If you own a major-brand bike and you're at a major race, you can probably get limited service at your manufacturer's team support van.

Thrasher: A daredevil mountain biker who rides fast, without much finesse.

Track: If you want to pass somebody and they won't let you go by, scream this word. Trail etiquette dictates that they give you right-of-way. As you pass, watch out for elbows. If somebody screams this at you, move aside.

Trials: A slow-speed event in which you ride your bike over rocks, dinosaurs, Volkswagens and almost anything else you can think of. If you don't put your foot down, you win.

Washboard: A patch of kidney-bouncing earth ripples. It's uncomfortable, but not really dangerous if you don't tighten up.

Washouts: This happens when water erodes a trail. Exposed rocks and other junk wait at the bottom to puncture your tires or send you flying.

Worlds: The world championships. Unlike the season-long Grundig or NORBA national series, which reward consistency, the Worlds are a one-day, winner-take-all event.

Credits

Bob Allen/Outside Images: pages 95, 112, 113, 114, 116

Donna Chiarelli: pages 6, 24

Joan Dwyer: page 126

Rich Etchberger: pages 62, 99, 100, 154, 159, 161, 162

Hiroyuki Kaijo/Singletrack: page 142

Ed Landrock/RSI: pages 118, 129

Tom Moran: Singletrack: pages 66, 151, 164, 167, 174, 182

Neal Palumbo/Singletrack: page 146

John Pratt/Pursuit Photo: pages 70, 71, 72

Carl Schneider: page 98

Mike Shaw: pages 23, 82, 110, 111

Walter Smith: pages 1, 36, 46, 50, 51

Index

Racing (*continued*)
  goals for, 167
  training, 170–77, 178–79
Rain, riding in, 123–25
"Ready" position, for
      clearing obstacles, 44,
      46, 141–42
Rear cables, 24
Relaxation, importance of, 3
  for climbing, 58
  for descending, 154
Responsible riding, environ-
      ment and, 26–28,
      128
Rest, in training routine, 172
Rey, Hans, 116
Riding conditions, antici-
      pating
  in daylight vs. darkness,
      140
  trail reading, 137–38
  in wet weather, 125
Rivet tool, 22, 96–97
Rock fields, dealing with,
      120–22
Rock Shox Quadra suspen-
      sion, 182
Rockwell, Myles, 161–63
Roman, Franck, 162–63

s

Saddle
  fore/aft position, 6–7
  height, 5–6
  remaining on, 94, 153
  tilt, 6
Safety guidelines, 34–35
Sand
  riding through, 97
  turning in, 146

Schrader valves, 24
Seat. *See* Saddle
Shifting, 13
Shimano components, 10,
      11, 183
Shocks. *See* Impact absorp-
      tion; Suspension bikes
Shoes, 17
  clipless pedals and, 93
Shopping guidelines, for
      bikes, 9–15
Sight-reading trails, 137–38
Singletrack, basic skills for,
      19
Singletrack stand, 89–90
Six-in-one tool, 22
Size of bike, importance of,
      5
Skidding
  environmental impact of,
      28
  preventing, 149
Skill drills
  braking, 150
  climbing, 153
  cornering, 148
  descending, 156
  obstacles, 138
  passing, 157
  stair riding, 116–17
  trail reading, 138
Slush, riding in, 131–32
Snow, riding in, 129–32
Spare tubes, 23–24
Specialized tires, 126,
      183
Speed, 77–80. *See also* Braking
  clearing obstacles and,
      43–44
  cornering and, 146
  curves and, 74–75, 76
  on descents, 68
  high, flat tires at, 113–15

rain and, 124
training for, 171–72
Speedplay pedals, 183
Spin, climbing and, 59
Spokes, 24
Sprints, for building speed, 172
Stairs, riding down, 116–17
Standing
in rock fields, 120
when climbing, 56–57
Steel bikes, 10
Stem, riding position and, 7
Steps, riding down, 116–17
Stretching, pros' views on, 161
Sunburn at high altitude, avoiding, 134
Suspension bikes, 11, 81–84, 182–83
Swenson, Peter, 137–38, 150, 153, 156
Switchbacks, nose wheelies and, 108–9
Sydor, Alison, 159

Tange Struts suspension, 182
Tanner, Todd, 150, 156
Team Cannondale, tips from, 158–63
Test rides, 13
Tilford, Steve, 156, 157
Tire levers, 23
Tires
descents and, 68
excessive air pressure in, 97
flat, at high speed, 113–15
folding, 25

mud and, 126
for racing, 183
Tire tubes. *See* Tubes, tire
Titanium bikes, 10
Toe strap, emergency uses for, 25
Tomac, John, 137, 153
Tools, essential, 22–25, 96–97, 180
Top tube and stem lengths, riding position and, 7
Trackstands, 89–90, 121
Traction
for climbing, 56, 61
rain and, 124
Trails
environmental impact on, 26–28
maintaining, 20
reading, 137–38
snow-covered, 131
Training for races, 170–72
advice from pros, 178–79
with heart rate monitor, 175–77
programs, 172–75, 179
Trash, cleaning up on trails, 27
Traveling with bike, 29–31
Tri-Flow lubricant, 16, 126
Tubes, tire, 27–28
half-filled, 182
spare, 23–24
Turns, strategies for, 73–76, 146–48

Uphill riding. *See* Climbing
Upper body, riding position and, 8

V-ditches, dealing with, 103–5
Vertigo, beginning riders and, 3–4
Vision, 25, 38–41, 94, 137–38. *See also* Night riding

Warranties, bike, need for, 14
Water. *See also* Fluids
 high-altitude riding and, 134
 physical need for, 96
 riding through, 97
Weather conditions
 rain, 123–25
 snow, 129–32
Weight of bike, importance of, 14
Weight shifting, 16
 for braking, 87
 for climbing, 151, 153

curves and, 75
 on suspension bikes, 81, 84
Wheelies, 45–48. *See also* Bunny-hops
 nose, 71–72, 108–9
Wiens, David, 145
Winter training, advice from pros, 162
Winter weather, riding in, 129–32
Women's bikes, choosing, 11
Wooden bridges, crossing in wet weather, 125
Wrenches, 23
Wrists, riding position and, 8

Yeti Pro FRO tires, 183